STOP WORRYING; START WRITING

HOW TO OVERCOME FEAR, SELF-DOUBT AND PROCRASTINATION

SARAH PAINTER

Siskin
Press

First published in Great Britain in 2017 by

SISKIN PRESS LIMTED

Copyright © 2017 by Sarah Painter

Cover Design: Inspired Cover Designs

This book is dedicated to the lovely listeners of The Worried Writer podcast. Thank you so much for joining me every month.

NOTE ON THE TEXT

I am British and this book is written in British English. For those who prefer to read in American English, I apologise, and hope that the alternative spelling and grammar isn't too off-putting.

Also, after researching the current style guides (and discovering that the topic is hotly debated!), I have followed the BBC, the *Guardian* and *The Financial Times* and written the noun 'internet' in lowercase throughout.

Finally, some portions of this text were originally published on the Worried Writer website. They are reproduced here in edited and extended form.

All quotes from my wonderful interviewees are included with their permission.

CONTENTS

INTRODUCTION

Hello and welcome. Thank you for picking up this book and, if you are a fellow worried writer, I hope you find it helpful.

Almost four years ago, my dream came true and I became a published author. Through denial and mind tricks and sheer stubbornness I had weathered seven years of rejection to reach the fabled land. I had what I had dreamed of my whole life; a publishing deal. I had achieved the goal which had consumed my every spare second and had kept me awake at night with desperate longing and the fear that I would never 'make it'.

However, instead of riding high on a cloud of happiness (although I had lots of moments which felt like that) I felt exposed and frightened, fraudulent and beset by doubt. My fear and anxiety didn't disappear the moment I was 'chosen'. In fact, in some areas it grew. Plus, I had a whole new set of worries to contend with: Was the book really good enough? Would people hate it? Hate me? On the night before publication day I was so terrified that I actually considered phoning my publisher and begging them not to release my book.

Also, I discovered that there were layers within the publishing industry. It was one thing to be intellectually aware there was a hierarchy which spanned from six-figure advances reported in the *Bookseller* and appearances on daytime television to low first-time author advances and digital-only distribution, and quite another to be inside it. Having said for years that I 'just wanted to be published' and I didn't care about the rest, I found, to my irritation, that I *did* care. It mattered because I had bound-up my sense of self-worth and success with my publishing deal. A cruel voice (spoiler alert – it was my voice!) whispered that I still wasn't a *real author*.

I had a tight deadline to deliver the second book and, through misery and self-doubt, I managed it, but it was not a joyful experience. After that, tired and anxious, my old habits of procrastination reappeared. These were closely followed by extended sessions of self-flagellation. ('Why are you so lazy?' 'You don't have what it takes.' 'You will never be a real author.') And I finished each day defeated and guilt-ridden.

Having always needed a certain amount of 'busy-ness' to keep procrastination at bay, I decided to add something else to my working week of writing fiction and blogging. I had become mildly obsessed with podcasts – particularly those which discussed the creative life – and I fancied the challenge of learning something new, so I decided to start The Worried Writer: A podcast to help writers to overcome fear, self-doubt, and procrastination. I figured I had some experiences and tips to share and a whole lot more to learn. What better way to do so than by asking other authors, most of whom were far more experienced and successful and productive than I?

The following two years, with many conversations both public and private, have been a revelation and I can hardly believe – or overstate – the difference in my writing life. Yes, I've achieved some external success in terms of new publishing deals, books sold, money made, but if my early experiences have taught me anything it is this: external rewards are never going to be enough. External validation will never silence your inner critic (and it shouldn't) and a fancy agent or big book deal or a nice review will never be more than a fleeting moment of 'yay'. If you don't clean up your own head-space, develop productive and healthy work habits, and value your own creativity and work *before* you are published (or get a massive deal or agent or win an award or whatever your own personal definition of 'made it' might be), it won't magically appear *after*. In fact, you may find that your insecurities grow in proportion to the size of your success.

I know.

Sorry.

Which leads me to my point... The external successes of the last four years make me very happy and proud, but I would not be writing this book (or, possibly, writing for publication at all) if I hadn't transformed my internal landscape. I am a work-in-progress and always will be; I still compare myself to others, get hurt by negative comments, and waste hours online when I should be writing but, and this is the key, I do all of those things a LOT less than before. And I'm happier and more productive in my writing life than I have ever been.

I hope this book can help you make similar changes, and that it makes you feel less alone in this writing lark.

Disclaimer

Before we get started, I want to talk about some of the language used in this book (no, not that sort – I've kept it pretty clean!). I am both a worried writer and a generally anxious person. When I speak about worries or anxieties (which I think of as 'worries with teeth') I am not referring to clinical anxiety.

I also have experience of living with an anxiety disorder and it is a different beast. It is not something that can be cured by positive mental attitude (although that can definitely help in the recovery stage) or something that you should take lightly. If you are suffering with panic attacks, uncontrollable negative thought patterns, or other symptoms that might be more than just 'worry', please do seek medical advice.

If you have already received a diagnosis for anxiety or depression (they often go together), please look after your mental health first. See your healthcare professional, locate a support group or counsellor, and talk to trusted friends and family.

Writing can be a wonderful escape, and even a type of therapy, but the last thing I want to do is to make anybody suffering with an illness feel worse, or as if they can cure themselves by 'forming a writing habit' or 'changing their mindset'.

Also, although I am sure this is obvious, I am not a doctor and nothing in this book constitutes medical advice.

1

EQUIP YOURSELF

I decided to start with this subject not only because it's logical, but because I think it's one of the simpler tasks and why not start with an easy win? When you are battling fear and self-doubt, taking small steps is the only way forward and, crucially, once you are moving it is easier to keep going.

It also includes an important shift in your thinking (something I am going to mention a lot throughout this book); you are going to start taking your writing – and yourself as a writer – seriously. Maybe you feel that you already do this but there is no harm in going over the basics.

So, in order to battle self-doubt and get your work done, you need to equip yourself correctly. If you wanted to become good at tennis, you would buy a decent racket; if you wanted to start watercolour painting, you would buy brushes, paint, and paper, and writing is no different.

The temptation is to say 'I already have a computer' and leave it at that, but there is so much more to this topic. By giving your writing set-up the time and attention it deserves, you are taking the first step to a new mindset. Make no mistake, equipping yourself is a mental exercise in taking your writing seriously and by undertaking it, you are also giving yourself permission to take it seriously; something that will have a greater effect that you can possibly imagine.

So, even if you already write regularly or consider yourself fully tooled-up, please skim over the following list and check in with your own set-up. Is it optimal? Have you given it the care it deserves?

Equipment check-list

As writers we are exceedingly lucky; our equipment is very cheap and, in some cases, available to borrow or share. If you can sensibly afford to do so, I recommend you spend a little bit of money as, in addition to being able to choose the right items for your needs, things that we pay for hold more emotional and motivational weight. On this subject, if you truly don't have any cash or have been given some of your writerly equipment, then please remember that you can do this for free but you need to invest something else to give the equipment its proper gravitas. Ask for one of the items for Christmas or as a birthday gift, assign a monetary value to the time you spend reading the book on writing (as if it were hours spent at your day job), and take notes when reading (or use post-it notes to mark pages). Signal to yourself that this is an active process of studying, not 'just' reading.

Essentials

Computer

There might be a few folk who still do all of their composition and editing using paper and pen, but the vast majority will require a computer for at least part of the process. You don't need anything fancy and, if you are reading this book, there is a good chance you already own something suitable.

If you are in the market for a writing-only computer, then prioritise the keyboard, as that needs to be responsive and comfortable. Maybe consider a solid-state machine as they are super-quick to boot up.

If you are interested, for the last few years I have been using Netbooks to write. They are portable, cheap, and have tiny memories so I cannot do much with them except write and send the occasional email. This suits me perfectly as I have an iMac in my office for everything else (image editing, website design, business administration).

Another tip is to buy a really cheap machine which is for writing only. A few authors, including romantic-comedy writer Clodagh Murphy, use an old-school word processor called the NEO. I bought one after interviewing Clodagh and it's very good for writing first-draft material. You can only see a few lines of text at a time, which discourages editing/reading and it does, literally, nothing else. I can't surf the net or play solitaire or do anything at all except write. Plus, it's very light, rugged, and runs on AA batteries (with an incredible battery life). I bought mine on eBay for around £30.

A place to write

In the short term, you can write anywhere. The kitchen table, sitting up in bed, the corner of a cafe. Long-term, however, using laptops on tables which are too tall or too low, slumping in bed, or using bad seating, will impact your health. I know too many writers who have suffered with RSI or back problems not to say, in my very best 'mum voice'; you must set up a good desk and chair in which to write.

This doesn't have to be expensive. I found my desk chair in a furniture-recycling place (it just needs to be adjustable and comfortable) and I spent £10 on a tilting footrest from an office-supply store. You can find guidelines for good computer set-up (screen in your eye line so that you aren't craning forward etc) online and there are ergonomic keyboards and mice if you are already suffering with pain in your wrists.

This is another area in which the timer method (more on that later in the book) can be excellent. If you do timed writing sessions of, say, thirty minutes each, with a five or ten minute break in between each one, then make sure you stand up and stretch/walk around the house for your breaks.

Books

As Stephen King famously said, to be a writer you must 'read a lot and write a lot.'

So, indulge your passion for reading guilt-free (and if you don't have a passion for reading, then kindly put this book down and choose a different career). The only thing I would add is that you should read widely and with enjoyment. Read what you enjoy for fun, read whatever takes your fancy, read what interests you.

This can be expensive, I know, but you can keep costs down by making full use of your local library (ours has a brilliant online-ordering facility) and second-hand bookshops (charity shops in the UK often have good book sections). Also, if you have heavy research requirements, know that you can probably use your local university's library. Either a free reader card will let you access the books on the premises or a small yearly fee might give you borrowing rights, too. Just ask!

Keep a record of all expenses (with receipts) as you may be able to claim these against tax if you sell your writing down the line.

Other things to consider

Books (and articles) on writing

Most writers I know love reading about writing. There are a minority, however, who absolutely do not – they find it stultifying and constricting. If you are one of these people (and you are happy with your writing and productivity) then please don't mess with your system – it's obviously working for you!

To everybody else, I say a few books on the craft of writing can be useful. The main thing to remember is that they are not rules, just guidelines. Each written from a particular writer's viewpoint (and filtered through their own experience, education, and personal process). Take what works for you and ignore what doesn't.

Sometimes, if I'm stuck in my WIP, I might read a few chapters of a book on plot and I will find it gives me an insight into the story I'm having trouble with. It's not even new information that I'm gathering, but it just reminds me of what I already know, or the particular place I am in makes me see old information in a new light. Bestselling thriller author C.L. Taylor is also a fan of books on writing. In the podcast, she explained:

'I think they are helpful when you're trying to clarify an idea and see if it's got legs... Whether it makes you think about structure or theme or character, I find there's always something in rereading those books during the very early stage of planning that helps me to remember all of the different elements I need to concentrate on. One of these days I need to go through those books and write down all of the bits that I end up rereading every single time I write a new book so that I've got them all in one place!'

I like reading about productivity, too, as I'm always looking for tips to improve my organisation and output. Taking a more 'business-like' approach to the craft of writing (focusing on timed writing sessions and so on), helps me to stop stressing over the quality of the work and just get on with it!

Courses

This is definitely not essential and I would caution against spending lots of money unless you are sure about what you are getting, but courses can be really useful. Not just for the information they provide, but for the community and mentoring aspect. Do your research before signing up for anything and make certain the course will provide what you want at a reasonable cost (look for reviews as well as vetting the teacher/course-provider).

Podcasts

If you have the technology (a smartphone, iPod, laptop, desktop, tablet) then these are free! There are lots of writing-related podcasts (such as the Worried Writer, ahem) available with tips and encouragement. They have the added bonus of being available to consume while you are doing other things! For example, I listen to writing, productivity, and business podcasts on my daily walk. I wouldn't be writing then anyway, so it doesn't cut into my creative time.

Other good opportunities include while driving, cleaning, or cooking.

Finally, a word of warning. Reading about writing and following courses on craft and researching can all, very easily, become methods of procrastination. There is a time for learning and it goes hand-in-hand with actually writing.

In the same vein, there is a time for story research:

- For a clearly-defined period before you begin.
- In short bursts while you write your story (making sure it doesn't interrupt your writing time).
- After you have written the book to make sure you haven't made big errors and to add pertinent detail to what you have already written.

Thinking about writing, talking about writing, reading about writing, and doing research for your story: None of these things count as writing and they should all be done AFTER you have got your words for the day!

2

BUILD THE HABIT

It is no exaggeration to say that everything changed for me when I realised just how powerful my daily habits were.

Early on, when I was very anxious about writing fiction, I used to spend hours and hours procrastinating to avoid the Word document. When I finally opened it, it was with an accompanying sense of desperation and misery (I had already wasted so much time! I was so rubbish!). Sometimes I never even got that far and I would write off the day, telling myself it was too late to get started and I would do better the following morning.

After months of this self-defeating and anxiety-ridden behaviour, I truly thought that I just wasn't disciplined enough to be a writer. I had the phrase 'writers write' written on a post-it note and I knew that I should 'just do it' but, while I had good days in which I managed to trick myself into writing, I wasn't making the progress that I dearly wanted.

I remember speaking to my friend (YA author and wonderful human being Keris Stainton) and feeling intense relief when she described 'sneaking up on her work'. We talked about our best time to write (first thing in the morning) and the intense joy (okay, relief) that came on a good day when we had completed our allotted words first thing and could spend the rest of the day with a sense of freedom.

It helped and I began prioritising writing first thing. I would sit up with the alarm and reach for my book (it had been my habit to read with my morning cuppa) and then force myself to open the laptop instead. I would say to myself, 'do you want to read another book or write one?'

So, I had made some changes, but I was inconsistent. As soon as I wasn't working on a particular project, I would revert to reading first thing. Or I would reward a 'good writing day' with the treat of reading in bed, rather than writing. Or with a day 'off'. Which often turned into a week or two weeks 'off'.

How To Build A Solid Writing Habit

I can't remember where I first heard about leveraging habits, but I know that, suddenly, a few people seemed to be talking about it on the podcasts and blogs I read (did I mention I have an addiction to reading about writing and productivity?). And something just clicked. I realised that it wasn't a case of being inherently lazy or undisciplined – I did several things every single day without even thinking about them and that this – the automatic action with zero waste of energy for decision-making (or dithering!) – was the key to the day-to-day life I wanted.

And this is it in a nutshell: making decisions is hard. It uses energy. If you imagine you start each day with a coffee mug full of mental energy (or willpower, if you prefer) and that every decision you make takes a spoonful from that mug, then you can see that it will – eventually – run out. This is why we often 'give in' and make unhealthy choices (like a bag of crisps with a big glass of wine) in the evening, seemingly sabotaging a halo-worthy day. We aren't fundamentally lacking in willpower – we've just used up our daily quota.

The good news, however, is that you can game the system. If you know that making decisions takes valuable spoonfuls of willpower, you can conserve them by MINIMISING THE DECISIONS YOU MAKE EVERY DAY.

This is where habits come in

Think about the stuff that you do every single day; watching television while you eat your breakfast, brushing your teeth, clearing the dishes after dinner, putting on your shoes before leaving the house... You don't have to think about these tasks – you don't have to make a conscious decision to do them – and you never (or hardly ever) miss them out. However ingrained and natural these behaviours feel, you weren't born doing them. Somewhere along the way, you developed the habit and now they are a part of your life.

Don't think of this as being boringly predictable, think of it as freeing up your precious mental energy for the really difficult or important or fun stuff!

How does this relate to writing?

You might be thinking that brushing your teeth doesn't take very long and writing a novel does, but you are going to build your writing habit by starting small. Even tiny actions, if they are repeated regularly over time, can have a big impact.

Plus, once you establish a habit it's easier to tweak it. For example, once you have a solid habit of writing for ten minutes every day during your lunch break, it is easier to increase that to fifteen minutes or thirty.

It's this last principle we're going to use to get started

Think of an existing habit you have and adjust it. For example, when you brush your teeth, use that time to think about your writing. If you don't have a story in mind, use the time to brainstorm ideas. If you're completely stuck, just use the time to reflect on your new creative habit. The focus should be on positivity; you are giving yourself permission to daydream, not trying to accomplish anything concrete or scary.

After a week or so, you are going to add a new habit and this one will actually involve writing. Pick a clearly-defined task that is easy to complete, and pick a time that is both easy to remember and suits your current schedule. The aim is to minimise every possible block to achieving the task and, once you've done it, to reward yourself. I like to use stickers for this, but it's your choice!

For example, you might decide to write for ten minutes every day (or every week day). That's a small, clearly defined task.

You might choose to add it to your evening routine, say after dinner (before you get up to wash the dishes) or first thing in the morning before you get out of bed.

Next, you prepare for success. If your writing session is scheduled for first thing in the morning, put your notebook and pen (or laptop) next to your bed the night before.

Repeat the habit for a few weeks until it feels very natural and easy. If you miss a session, don't beat yourself up about it, just do the next one.

One final note: Even if you're finding your goal very easy to manage, don't be tempted to increase or change it too quickly. If you raise the bar too fast, you're more likely to miss sessions and get discouraged. Allow yourself to 'win' at the task easily and regularly and you'll soon have an instinctual writing habit in place.

If you want to read more on building a writing habit, I recommend Chris Fox's book *Lifelong Writing Habit* or, for a more in-depth look at the subject, try *The Power of Habit: Why We Do What We Do And How To Change* by Charles Duhigg.

In case you need more evidence for the value of a daily writing habit: Bestselling thriller and crime author Mel Sherratt found that switching to writing every day (as opposed to binge writing for a couple of weeks and then leaving it) fundamental in increasing her productivity.

'I try to get 2000 words done before breakfast every morning. It doesn't always work, but I try, especially if I'm drafting, to get that out of the way... I feel like that starts me off for the day and if I don't do it first thing in the morning then I will be the worst procrastinator... Once I've done those I feel much better about myself and I'll carry on with more words or more editing, depending on which part of the process I'm at...

'I used to be a person who writes, say, 20,000 words in a week... and then leaves it for a while before coming back to it. But now I'm starting to learn that it's better to write every day; even to write a couple of hundred words every day helps to keep you in the story.'

Key Points:

- Making decisions takes energy so use habits and routine to minimise the decisions you have to make.
- Write first thing in the morning (if at all possible) before the day wears you down/you are derailed by other responsibilities.
- Make writing a daily habit.

3

MAKE FRIENDS WITH YOUR WORRIES

As a professionally diagnosed, card-carrying, 'actually sometimes properly unwell', anxious person, I have an instinctive dislike of phrases like 'make friends with anxiety'. I used to think that they were misunderstanding the nature of the condition and were about to tell me I should be grateful for it or some such nonsense.

However, over the years I have realised two very important truths; my anxiety is not me and my anxiety will always be with me.

In accepting that it isn't me (or, more accurately, all of me – like all of us, I am more complex and vast and change-able than one adverb or diagnosis can possibly contain) I feel strong and hopeful. And by accepting that it will always be with me, tugging on my sleeve and shouting warnings, I feel calmer and more in control of the situation. This is how it is, I say to myself; I am these two things. Confident enough to think that I have stories worth telling and the hubris to write them down for others to read, and insecure enough to – simultaneously – feel that I am worthless and talentless.

My anxiety is always around. Sometimes she's quiet (oh,

joy!) and sometimes she's just a small voice, but sometimes she elbows her way to the front, sits on my chest, and demands my full attention. By imagining my anxiety in this way – as a separate creature, I am continually aware of her limitations and my own power. By which I mean I can send her to sit in the corner when she is stopping me from doing what I want. I can thank her for caring about me and trying, in her own inept way, to protect me (which is, of course, what my anxiety is always trying to do), and then tell that I have acknowledged her fears but she needs to shush now because I am working.

Elizabeth Gilbert writes beautifully about this in her book on creativity, *Big Magic*. I've popped the details in the further reading section at the back of the book, if you are interested.

Recently, I went a step further and began picturing my anxiety as a small creature – a little blue dragon with a worried expression, to be precise. It felt silly to start with and, to be honest, if capital 'A' anxiety really ramps up then it is hard to maintain the illusion, but for normal days it really works and, I believe, it helps it from growing into the more terrifying monster of anxiety disorder which plagues me from time to time.

So, however daft you might feel, try picturing your anxiety (or the negative voice which plagues you) as a cute little critter. You know the kind of thing – goofy but adorable. Making it into something adorable and cute diffuses some of its power (making it inherently less alarming), and makes me feel better about its permanent residency in my life.

Accepting that my worries will always be there has enabled me to use them to my advantage. If I want extra motivation, I imagine giving my little worry dragon something to worry about (as it were). I might say to my anxiety, 'Hey, I know you're worried that this book I'm writing is rubbish and I will ruin my career and disappoint my readers and die alone and unloved in a ditch, but I think not writing it would be even worse. Imagine that – I'd die alone and unloved in a ditch with the ADDED REGRET OF NOT HAVING PURSUED MY LIFE'S PASSION. IMAGINE THE REGRET!' Now my worry dragon is working for me, not against.

The other thing to remember is something I allude to at the start of this chapter. That our anxiety is trying to protect us. The fear of failure that rears up and stops us from finishing a book is a self-defence mechanism. If we don't finish the work we cannot send it out to be judged (or read it as a completed story and judge it ourselves). The anxious voice (my little worry dragon!) which says 'you can't make a podcast because you will sound stupid and people will hear your horrible voice' thinks it is doing me a favour. It hates change. It hates fear. It hates risk. And all because it wants me to stay safe.

My worry dragon is always on duty and always has my best interests at heart, but it isn't a very nuanced being. It cannot differentiate between 'fear' and 'excitement'. It gets them confused. It also can't differentiate between 'nerves because I'm going to do something a little bit scary that is also a bit exciting and will almost certainly be really brilliant' and 'Argh! It's a lion. Run! Run for your life!'.

Yes, this voice – that we all have to a greater or lesser extent – has been passed down to us from generations of surviving ancestors. People who were smart enough not to avoid risk long enough to make babies and successfully rear them to adulthood. We are, quite literally, *bred* to be frightened. The problem is that the world has changed dramatically in a short space of time and evolution is a slow old process. This means our hind brain (our primitive, instinctual area) is ill-equipped to identify danger in the modern world. It is still pretty fabulous at stopping us from wandering over the edges of cliffs, out into speeding traffic, and from picking up pointy objects firmly by the sharp end, but it's less great at sorting out the mortal-danger wheat from the humdrum chaff.

Further complicating matters, our danger-meter is reacting to all kinds of things – the over-stimulation of bright lights, noisy traffic, crowds of commuters on the train, rolling news headlines, illuminated screens, work stress – as if they are about to bite our heads off. No wonder it starts to complain when we try to do things which add to this background terror and spike our adrenaline. No wonder many of us feel tired and a bit fearful a lot of the time!

I have found recognising all of this hugely helpful. It enables me to be kinder to myself in general, and when I'm feeling feeble or frightened of a seemingly simple task such as driving somewhere new or making a phone call, I am more able to talk myself 'down' from those feelings of anxiety. When you know that your worry dragon is trying to protect you from harm, you can talk to it more effectively and the knowledge of what is really going on can be liberating. When I used to try to shut down the voice completely, it just got worse.

Another good tip is to set a time for worry. Then, whenever you get that negative voice or worry you can nod and say 'thanks, I'll think about that during worry time'. Then, at your appointed time (more scheduling!) and for your allotted time only, you allow yourself to worry. Go nuts! At first, you might want to allow half an hour (or even an hour) for this, especially if you are very anxious but, over time, you will probably find that you need less and less worry time. I don't use this technique all the time, but when my anxiety is flaring up and my worry dragon is resisting the gentle requests to sit quietly in the corner, I find that deferring the worries to the allotted time can do the trick. It's the deferment, the containment, and the sense of control which are the magic in this, not the specific details, so feel free to adjust the process until it works for you. You could, for example, set a 'worry hour' for a Sunday afternoon rather than having one every day.

Hopefully these suggestions will help but, as I said in the introduction, if you find that you feel anxious a lot of the time and it is affecting your happiness and quality of life, please seek medical advice. You are not weak or silly and there is help available if you need it.

To bring things back to writing – recognising that your worry dragon is only trying to protect you might lead to the question 'what is it protecting me from?'. Writing and publishing isn't life-threatening, after all. However, your worry dragon doesn't know this. It wants to protect you from all harm (and it can't tell imagined fears from real ones, emotional anxiety from lethal danger). Think of it as loving, but not all that bright. Give it a pat on the head and get back to work.

4

PRACTICE NOT PRODUCT

Here's the thing. Nobody expects to pick up an electric guitar for the first time and crank out a perfect rendition of Hendrix's 'All Along The Watchtower' and nobody starts a painting class with the aim of reproducing a Monet-level masterpiece, but writers around the world scribble a few sentences or chapters and are then surprised – and disheartened – when they aren't as good as their favourite novelist.

There are lots of reasons for this; most of us use words and writing every day (emails, speech, work reports, essays for college, shopping lists) so we have a false idea of our own expertise. We love reading books and feel that we must have absorbed, by osmosis, the ability to write our own. Plus, we have been seduced by the idea of talent or genius and read enough, usually over-simplified, 'overnight success' stories to believe that a first attempt can yield gold.

I had the same feeling. I distinctly remember thinking (and have verified it by reading my angst-ridden diary of the time) 'what if I try to write and there is nothing there? What if I try and I can't do it?' The dream that I might, one day, 'be' a writer would be taken away forever.

If it hadn't been the fear of never finding out, with an

approaching milestone birthday to add spice to the mix, I might never have found the courage to try and that thought gives me proper chills.

I was, I can see now, making the classic mistake of thinking that writing talent was something I either had or didn't have; a fixed quantity. I had absorbed the notion of The Writer (note the capital letters) as a born genius, a natural creative, an almost other-worldly being who had been anointed by the muses and chosen for a literary career.

What saved me, and I hope will save you too, is the realisation that there was another path. It wasn't the path of the artist (although high art can still be produced), it was the path of the craftsperson.

I read about the importance of work and sustained effort, of daily routine and word count goals, and I realised something wonderful – hard work trumped natural talent every single time. Rather than worrying about whether I had the special feather of literary greatness I could, instead, find out whether I had a work ethic, self-discipline, willpower. I was pretty sure I did have those things, to be honest, and as soon as I had a clear path ahead I was able to take those first steps.

I'm not discounting talent, of course; it always helps! And some people are definitely natural-born storytellers or wordsmiths, while others have to work at their craft for a lot longer than others (life, as ever, is not fair). I do think that there needs to be some sort of innate ability or facility for expressing yourself in writing and for creating characters and story, but I also believe that innate ability is just a tiny seed. What matters is whether you nurture that seed.

And, for the record, I would choose the ability to work hard over natural talent every day of the week. Without the former, the latter is almost useless.

Where is all this leading? To the focus on practice (the 'hard work') over product.

Prioritise Process

If you focus on the end result (a finished novel or, worse yet, a *good* finished novel) you have a very long and lonely road ahead. Days and weeks and months, maybe even years, before you achieve something. Focus on today instead. What counts as a win today? An hour of writing? One hundred new words? Opening your document and thinking about your story?

This isn't just a practical solution, it's a vital mindset shift. If you don't enjoy, prioritise, and celebrate the daily work, you're going to have a miserable time as a writer. And, ultimately, the daily work is what being a writer is all about. If you don't enjoy – or at least find satisfaction – in the process, why not spend your time doing something else?

The other thing about process versus product is this: It lets you practice. If you let go of the result (the short story, screenplay or novel), you are free to experiment with your writing. You can write crappy scenes knowing that they will probably not get used in your final product but not feel frustrated. You know that the practice is the thing. Shifting the focus to the practice will ease the pressure of perfection, while making sure you are doing the very thing that will help you improve.

Mental Toughness

I have thought about productivity and forming good writing habits a lot, and researched the subject extensively for the last decade. I've read productivity books from different disciplines (entrepreneurs and self-help gurus) to see if there are tips and skills which can transfer to the author life. There comes a point in every productivity book I have read (and I have read many!) when the advice boils down to 'just do it'. And this is that point.

Nobody is going to make you practise your writing.

Nobody is going to care if you never get down to it and work on your craft and finish your book.

Nobody, that is, except you... So, start practising.

5

SET GOALS

I can still remember the moment when I fully grasped that truly, almost anything in life was possible if I set it as a goal and then made a plan by breaking it into smaller tasks. Once you have a map to follow with small, achievable steps you can just work through them until you arrive at your destination.

However, if you find this strategy makes you focus too much on product rather than practice (as discussed in the previous chapter) then please leave it for now to revisit at a later stage. Personally, I find that making a plan which I then follow helps me not to get overwhelmed by the enormity of the task (such as writing a 100,000 word novel) or the scariness of a task (self-publishing this book, for example). By focusing on each small step and ticking them off the list, the goal becomes an intellectual exercise; a series of tasks, rather than the big, terrifying sum of its parts.

When I decided to get my first novel, *The Language of Spells*, made into an audio book, I did my research and decided how I was going to approach it. Next, I wrote a list of everything I needed to do (commission a cover design, find a narrator, and so on) and then worked out the most logical order in which to tackle them. Some things, such as checking my contract to confirm that I definitely owned the audio rights and speaking to my agent had to come first, and then I slotted in the other tasks as seemed appropriate. Then I set a deadline and worked out approximate miniature deadlines for the other tasks, re-jigging the order as necessary.

Setting a firm deadline and a timeline for your list is vitally important, otherwise it will simply languish.

Take writing a novel. First off you set a word count for the project – let's say 90,000 words. Then you have a choice: You can either set a deadline and then work out how much you need to write per day/week in order to hit that deadline, or you decide what is a reasonable rate of writing (for you, don't be swayed by what others do) and work out when you will reach your final total.

For example, let's say you usually manage 1000 words in a good writing session. If you plan five of those a week, you would set your deadline for 18 weeks time (18 x 5000 = 90,000). Perhaps you look at your diary and see that you have a holiday booked in that time, so you add a week or two to give yourself that time off. Once you have set your schedule, check in with yourself. How do you feel? Nervous but excited? Great! Panicky and overwhelmed? Not so good… Revisit the schedule and play with the numbers until you hit a combination that feels good. You want it to feel like a challenge, but not completely impossible.

Once you are happy with your goal and your schedule, you need to help yourself to stick to it. Set up a system to keep track of your progress (I like to use one with small rewards, like a sticker chart!) and then stick to it. On days when you slip (and you will), don't add on the word count to the next day, as that will demotivate you very quickly; simply keep going as if the slip didn't happen. For example, let's say your daily target is 500 words and you miss a day. Don't think 'oh no, now I have to do 1000 today or I will be behind'. Simply shrug your shoulders and say 'today I'm going to get my 500 words' and then, when you do, celebrate! Pat yourself on the back, and mark the progress on your sticker chart or in your diary or whatever method you are using. Over time, the occasional missed day won't make much difference. If you don't put pressure on yourself, I would argue you are more likely to 'accidentally' catch up. There will be days when you go over your 500 words target and, as you get closer to the end of your book, you might find that you naturally speed up a bit. However, let's say you never catch up on those missed words. Worst case scenario – you finish your novel in twenty weeks instead of eighteen (or twenty-one weeks or twenty-two). You will still have finished your novel and achieved your goal.

It might feel counter-intuitive but productivity is usually improved by being kinder to yourself, not harsher. I discovered this after reading Hillary Rettig's excellent book, *The Seven Secrets of the Highly Prolific*. She recommends something which I found truly groundbreaking and, if you have a similarly perfectionist/control freak personality, you might find the same thing. Rettig says that rather than calling myself 'lazy' for not working, I should celebrate when I do! Positive reinforcement rather than an endless guilt-cycle of 'why are you so rubbish?'. I urge you to read the book, but I want to add my own experience because even though I found her advice liberating and wonderful, I didn't really believe it. I could see that it made sense and outwardly I said 'oh, yes, I deserve to be nicer to myself' and (imagine a little nervous laughter here), 'at least my working days would be more pleasant.' But deep down, I didn't believe that anything short of the big stick I used to beat myself would ever 'work'. Anyway, for the record: kindness absolutely works. And my work days are so much more enjoyable. (I know, duh!)

Finally, a word on motivation. When you set your goals they should reflect your larger definition of success. If you've properly thought this through and your goals are true – in that they truly reflect what you want to achieve and are part of your model for 'success', then (funnily enough) they will be much easier to achieve. When you hit a 'can't be bothered' day, you will be able to look at your goal (and your overall plan) and remember *why* you decided to write 500 words a day, or whatever it might be, and this might be enough to send you back to the keyboard.

The why is super-important. When you set your goals, interrogate them – do they support your definition of success? How will they help you to get there? How do you feel about the goal? Imagine how you will feel when you achieve it. Spend time on this and journal your findings. You are building castles out of thin air with your imagination and your will so take your time to make the foundations strong and true.

For example, if you have decided that your definition of success is to make £1000 a month from your writing and to get positive responses from readers (through messages or reviews) then your goals should relate to that ultimate aim. If regular money is your top priority then you will focus on the best – most controllable – way to achieve this, which is likely to be self-publishing (or being a hybrid author – published both traditionally and independently) and writing in one of the commercially successful genres such as romance or crime.

If, on the other hand, the top items on your definition of success are to win a literary prize and to see your novel in a bookshop then your best bet, goal-wise, is to pursue a traditional publishing deal and to work on a book which falls within the literary genre.

Although this exercise starts in broad strokes (literary versus commercial!), you can refine it with as much detail as you want. As long as you rank your priorities, which will tell you which projects should take most of your time and which might have to be done as 'hobby projects' or kept for a later date, you can fulfil a spectrum of desires.

For example, Mark McGuinness runs a successful creative coaching business and writes non-fiction titles within this niche. He fulfils his definition for success by making a living wage from his business, helping others (through his coaching and books), and working hours which allow him time with his family and time to write poetry. Those last two do not have financial goals attached, but they fulfil Mark's personal ambition to have quality family time, and his creative desire to write poetry. Mark has written about defining your own priorities in his book, *Motivation For Creative People*, and when we spoke, he explained how important our core values are to our motivation (which relates, of course, to the goals we set and our definition of success). Mark said:

> 'It's really important that your actions and your life are aligned with your values.'

Making sure your goals are in line with what you truly want (and truly value) as opposed to what you think you 'should' want or want to do, they will become supercharged with meaning and so much easier to follow. In fact, while we all have 'can't be bothered' days, if you are continually finding it difficult to stick to your new habits and schedule and to get the tasks done on your list, this might be a warning sign that you have set goals you don't truly desire. Maybe revisiting your internal set of values and priorities will be the key to unlocking your motivation.

Key Points:

- Set a concrete goal and then split it into small, manageable steps.
- Track your progress and reward every success.
- Don't worry about small slips or missed days in your schedule. Just keep on going.
- Make sure your goals are what you truly desire and value, not what you think you 'should' want to do.
- Revisit your goals regularly and don't be afraid to change course.

6

TRICK YOURSELF

There are so many mind games I play in order to get the work done. I have tried loads over the years, and kept the ones which work. I describe as many as possible in this chapter so that you can pick what works for you and discard the rest.

If you are having a instinctual reaction against the idea of 'needing' mind games (somebody once said to me 'why don't you just use willpower?'), then I urge you to take a moment before you reject my suggestions entirely. Sometimes we have a kneejerk reaction against the things which will be most powerful for us. Sometimes this is our old friend The Fear, trying to protect us from possible future discomfort, or because we are carrying baggage around which tells us that we 'don't deserve' help and that anything which uses the word 'trick' is a cheat and not worthy of a True Artist. I suggest you spend a few minutes exploring your reaction and why it is so strongly negative. It might be illuminating.

So, mind games. First off, I lie to myself and I highly recommend this strategy. When I am starting a first draft I tell myself it is just for fun (regardless of my true plans for the book – which might be extensive and ambitious). I tell myself that I am just going to tell a story, entertain myself, play around. I tell myself that it is totally private and that nobody will ever see the words I am writing. This is enormously freeing.

In the later stages of the book, during rewrites and final editing, I might have to change the lie. It might become 'this is just an intellectual exercise to see if I can improve my story' or 'practise my craft'. Conversely, by removing as many of the big picture (and scary!) things from the work, I am free to focus on it more keenly, to work harder on it and, crucially, to allow my creative voice free reign.

Another mind game is to trick myself into writing before I can put up barriers. One key strategy was to begin writing first thing in the morning, before I am fully awake. This way, my subconscious creativity is much closer to the surface and I am full of energy (willpower) to get started. Other ways to trick myself include putting on loud music (or white noise or weather sounds) which seem to distract my brain just enough to get me into the right state.

Using a timer. If I am feeling particularly feeble, I use timed sessions. I can tell myself that I'm only going to write for twenty minutes and the shame of not even doing twenty minutes of writing is enough to make me do it. I recommend this technique to anybody, at any stage of their writing career, and at any point in their process – it works for brainstorming, outlining, first drafting, and editing. Having honed the concept, I recommend a physical timer rather than one on your computer.

Tell yourself it is okay to write rubbish. As Julie Cohen said:

'What beginning writers don't know is that writing is mostly a process of failing... I think a crap first draft is pretty important.'

I find this advice truly liberating and I hope you do, too.

The problem with writers is that we are – first and foremost – readers. Or at least we should be! This means that we have spent our lives devouring published, edited, slaved-over prose. No wonder it is a horrible shock when we begin to write our own first drafts. Of course they are rubbish! Of course they are unpolished and clunky and full of plot holes the size of small planets.

Using multiple versions. I save a new version of my draft with ridiculous regularity. This means that I know I can always reverse a day (or two) of writing by skipping back to a previous version of the story. I hardly ever actually do this, but knowing that I can, that I am adding to a new 'just for today' version frees me to work on it.

Notes for more experienced writers!

Once you have finished and edited and released your third or fourth or fifth book, you might start to bemoan the 'vomit draft' method. You might start to wish that editing didn't have to be so damn hard.

The good news is that you will probably find that (for some of your books, at least) the editing does get easier. Your first drafts, however rough and ready, are likely to be better as you improve as a writer. You are more practised which makes you more proficient. You are more experienced about what needs to go into a book to make it book-shaped and you will, unconsciously, begin to add more of this structure and conflict to your early drafts.

The other good news is that you can try a little planning

or outlining (or brainstorming with coloured pens and a mind-map) and see if it suits you better than it did when you tried it back in your early days. Doesn't work? Why not try working on your first draft a bit more as you go along. Write in scenes rather than fragments and try to make sure each scene 'works' before moving on. A really good book which explains this method is Dean Wesley Smith's *Writing Into The Dark*.

Of course, you might find that these approaches stop you in your tracks or drain the joy from the first draft. If so, go back to wild and free drafting and don't worry about it.

A quick note on your developing skills as a writer

The bad news is that your awareness of craft will improve right alongside your skill, so you might not feel you are getting better. The more you know, the more you will find to criticise. Also, you may well be pushing yourself to write deeper, more complex books or to challenge yourself with different narrative forms or genres. While this is a positive thing, it will feel as if you are still at the bottom of the learning curve, rather than sitting at the top of it, feeling smug. Sorry! On the plus side, you will be writing better books and learning and growing as a writer.

Lying to yourself is an excellent strategy for all stages of writing and publishing. When facing an editorial letter, I save a new version of the document (so the old one is kept pristine and untampered-with) and I tell myself that I'm 'just going to try a few things'. This takes the pressure from the edits and stops me panicking that I am irrevocably breaking my book. I know that I have the original version, so it doesn't matter.

On the importance of fun

Another important mind game or trick is the exact opposite of my suggestion to treat writing seriously. When you are starting out, I argue that calling your writing 'work' will help you to prioritise it and to protect the time it takes in your busy life. It will help you to invest in your writing (to buy the computer, good desk chair and writing books that you require) and to keep going when you don't feel like it. You are taking it seriously, goddammit, so you will glue your backside to the chair and hammer out those words like a professional!

However, as time goes on, this approach can whip around and bite you. When the writing is 'work' it can no longer feel like fun. It gets weightier and weightier and, with the pressures of the publishing world (or, if you are relying on your writing income whether part-time or full-time, the financial pressure) can make it feel more onerous until you actively start to avoid it.

Before you know it, you are dragging yourself to the keyboard as if it is the hardest, most boring task in the world. What started as your delicious, private escape has become the working week.

To anyone pre-publication reading this, I can only apologise. I know how 'my diamond shoes are too tight' this sounds and I can only suggest that you skip this section. For the record, I know how fortunate I am to write full-time and I thank my lucky stars every single day. There are, however, real psychological issues with turning our passion/hobby into paying work and I want to make it clear to any others who might have gone full-time, only to find that they spend all day on social media, rather than writing, that they are not alone.

The way I have counteracted this is to remind myself

(continually!) that the writing is the fun bit. I started to say (both in my head and out loud to my husband, the lucky duck) that I 'get to' write in the morning rather than 'I must' and I try to only think of administration and marketing activities as 'work' and the creative writing bit as 'fun'. This is an ongoing process but it has definitely helped!

Key Points:

- Tell yourself whatever lies are necessary!
- Trick yourself into writing before fear can take hold (first thing in the morning or by blasting loud music).
- Use a timer for twenty-minute writing sessions.
- Save multiple versions so that you can always go back.
- Remember that you are improving, even when it doesn't feel like it!
- Remind yourself that it is fun. You are just making up stories, after all…

7

GET A SPECIAL WRITING HAT

Right, this tip might sound a little mad, but bear with me…

Like most (all?) of us, I was a bookworm as a child. Reading was my preferred activity, libraries were magical, and I reread my favourite books so often I could recite whole passages. As soon as I grasped that an actual person was behind the stories I escaped into at every available moment, I wanted to be a writer. Along with the desire, though, was the certain feeling that authors were more than just mere mortals. They were special.

Stories are magic so it was logical that Noel Streatfield, Nicolas Fisk, Enid Blyton, Judy Blume et al must also be, if not full-blown wizards, then certainly a breed apart.

Rather than being put sensibly aside as I grew older and wiser, this conviction grew with me. By the time I was a teenager and was reading everything from Charlotte Brontë and George Orwell to Stephen King and Joanna Trollope (via the eye-opening Erica Jong and the comforting brilliance of Terry Pratchett), my subconscious had deduced that authors were incredibly clever, erudite, glamorous, interesting, and confident. They knew things. They had lived. They had authority and a kind of stardust clung to their presence. If they weren't intimidatingly educated (Oxbridge), they were natural geniuses, beloved the world over for their innate talent. If they weren't lauded by the literary establishment, they were massively successful and dizzyingly prolific.

All of which is to say I put off writing for many years because I felt inadequate. How could I possibly measure up to these giants? Who was I, normal boring Sarah with her average degree and non-glamorous life and continual self-doubt (more the opposite of that bravery, that dashing self-confidence, I could scarcely imagine), to attempt to write a book?

Which leads me to the hat. Pick one of your writing heroes. Not a recent one, not one whose blog you follow and writing tips you read. Not someone from the realistic, adult world, but one from further back. A writer who got their hooks into your subconscious back when you were a dreamer, a player of games, a puddle jumper, a free thinker.

For all that I expound goals and schedules and tips and word counts and learning the business of writing as well as the craft, I still believe in the magic of writing and the magic of creativity. I also believe that we all have it. You have it. I have it. We just have to access it.

So, picture your writing hero. I chose Terry Pratchett because I have been reading his books since I was fourteen and, although I have greedily devoured his every word on the practice of writing, he embodies both my youthful enthusiasm and dreams and the happy productivity I aspire to in adulthood.

So, while you are picturing your chosen writer, hopefully you are getting a rush of feelings from your connection with them and their books and your memories of being curled up reading their words. That writer might not have a hat but might wear flamboyant clothes or a long scarf or they might have an outrageous beard (Terry Pratchett always wore a hat in public which is what kicked off my obsession with author hats). Pick one of their accessories or features or just imagine them wearing the mystical author hat. Now you are going to picture them giving you your own hat. Passing an extra baton (while keeping their own, there's room for everyone, not only a few slots available). Take the hat (literal or metaphorical, I have an actual top hat) and place it on your own head.

If you are still reading, thank you for your patience. I have no idea whether this will be helpful to anybody else but I know that I found it immensely cheering. In an uncertain profession with no recognised career path, an imaginary 'swearing-in' ceremony is less bonkers than it might sound. And, once you have your special writer's hat (real or imaginary, it doesn't matter) it will be there for you in times of stress. Perhaps you will don it every time you sit at the keyboard, perhaps you will keep it for feeble days and times of crisis to give you a little boost, to remind you of your indoctrination into The Author's Guild. Your hat will remind you that thousands before you have struggled with plot points and character motivation and finding just the right imagery or word and you are part of a grand tradition. Perhaps a tiny spark of that good feeling you had as a bookworm child will remind you of why you are doing this difficult and frustrating thing and that will help, too.

Another wonderful thing about the author's hat is that it helps you to separate your private self from your author self. One reason (probably the main reason) that writing is so hard is that it is exposing. We are taking our secret private thoughts and putting them out into the world. Yes, we are writing fiction and so it is our characters doing things and having conversations and murdering each other, but everybody knows that we direct our characters so they are *our* words and thoughts. Yes, it is a story, but what kind of sick-and-twisted (or stupid or shallow or clichéd) mind came up with that story, hmm?

So, yes. It's fraught. It's scary. We fear judgement and we fear exposure. We are opening our minds and our souls and inviting the world to take a peek (and to leave a nifty star rating on the internet!).

Something I have found vital in surviving this experience has been separating my writer self from my self-self. Yes, I am fully aware we are one and the same being, but it helps nonetheless and it might help you, too. When submitting to agents, for example, the only way I could manage to post my baby manuscript (with all the hopes and dreams, toil and sweat it represented) was by taking a very business-like approach and automating the whole thing. I decided how many subs would be out at any time (I chose three) and I kept a spreadsheet where I recorded responses (form rejection, personal rejection, request for more), and whenever a rejection came in, I simply sent out the next submission on my list so that I still had three 'out there'.

When I did the submissions I wore my author hat (metaphorically; I hadn't earned enough to buy an actual hat at this point). I knew that all writers got rejections, it was a rite of passage (just look at J.K! Stephen King papered his room with rejection slips!) so I embraced that tradition, plonked the hat on my head and got on with it. As the rejections came in, the author-me was more able to deal with them as an inevitable step on the road and as a comment on that particular project, while the personal me-me would have been utterly crushed and unable to lift my head for the following week.

Now, in all likelihood you are a more robust specimen. I did start this book with the premise that if I can do this, anybody can and perhaps you now see the extent to which I meant those words. I truly am a bowl of jelly. But I do think that rejection is hard for all of us and the fear of rejection and failure can make us procrastinate if not outright avoid certain essential steps. And I share my own experience just in case you, dear reader, have moments in which you are as feeble as me.

Putting ourselves 'out there'

You might think that the submission stage is the only time at which you will fear rejection and that once you are published, you will never face those fears again. If you are pre-publication and don't wish to be alarmed, look away now, but to the rest of you I share a knowing look of sympathy… It Never Ends.

Submitting to agents leads to the terror of an agent actually reading your work which leads to the terror of being taken on and having to discuss your work and edit it with that agent which leads to publishers reading (and rejecting and discussing and editing), which leads to readers reading and reviewing and emailing you.

Plus, once you are published (whether via the traditional route or independently) you will need to market your books, which involves social media, blogging, and being interviewed on websites and podcasts, as well as the possibility of print media, radio interviews, appearances at events, book launches, and even television (pause, while I faint at the mere thought).

When I first started blogging as Sarah Painter, author, I found it suddenly difficult. I had blogged before and written extensively for online and print publications in my previous career as a freelance journalist, but this was a new challenge. I knew that I wanted to be authentic and real, but I also felt nervous and exposed and uncertain as to how much of myself and my life I wanted to be public. As I already felt incredibly vulnerable through my fiction being available to the world, it felt too much to have to write about myself, too. Having a metaphorical 'hat' to put on really helped with those feelings. Once I was wearing the hat, I was able to gain a little perspective and to make certain rules about what I would and would not share publicly, and setting these boundaries (never mentioning my children by name or using photographs of them, for example) helped me to feel more in control.

8

MAKE THE TIME

Hands up if you've ever said (or heard someone say): 'I'd like to write a novel but I don't have the time.'

Writing seems to be on a lot of people's wish lists and I understand that perfectly – books are awesome, after all. For most, though, it remains just that; an item on a bucket list, sandwiched between swimming with dolphins and eating Fugu.

However, since you're reading this, I assume you're ready to take the first step to making your dream a reality. Or, perhaps, you've been writing for a while, but are frustrated by your lack of progress, the way months and years slip by and your work-in-progress still, stubbornly, refuses to limp over the finish line.

I apologise in advance, but this is not going to be a cuddly chapter with gentle advice because the hard truth is this: if you want to write, you make the time.

Or, to put it another way, if you don't make the time you will never write a novel. Let that sink in… Say it out loud if necessary:

If you don't MAKE the time you will NEVER write a novel.

How do you feel?

Assuming you're still reading, here are some tips on finding the time:

Stop watching television. Okay, maybe that's a little drastic, but consider your viewing habits. Do you spend three hours of an evening flicking through the channels? Do you regularly get 'caught' by a film or programme you don't really want to watch but end up seeing through to the end anyway? Replace this with one episode of something you really love (DVD box sets and Netflix were made for this!) and use the remaining two hours to write. As you can probably imagine, this technique works especially well if you do your writing hours first!

Set your alarm an hour earlier in the morning. Even allowing time to make an extra cup of tea or coffee to make the early start more palatable, you'll create fifty-five minutes of pure, uninterrupted writing time. Brilliant! Night owls, of course, could go to bed an hour later instead.

If you work full-time and/or have a family, you might have to cut something out of your life. What do you do on the weekends? I'm not saying that you can't have other interests but, in the short term at least, other hobbies may have to take a backseat so that you can dedicate one day a week to writing.

Examine your week for hidden opportunities. If you commute, you could write on the train or bus. If you drive to work, perhaps you could use the time to think about your WIP, keeping the story fresh in your mind and making it easier to keep working on it.

If you have young children, then ignoring the cleaning and using their nap time to write is essential. If they're older and you've reached the parent-as-taxi stage, then carry a notebook or tablet with you so that you can write while waiting for them during sport or music lessons.

. . .

Start saying 'no'. If you want to make the time to write, you're going to have to make it a priority. I'm not suggesting you live the life of a hermit, but you will need to turn down some social invitations. Don't worry, your true friends will understand and will be cheering you on.

Saying 'no' also applies to as many non-essential responsibilities as possible, and, most importantly, perfectionism. You can't do everything. Nobody can. Release yourself from the shackles of 'doing everything' right now as nobody else will do this for you. If you find it difficult to cut back on housework or extra-credit parenting tasks such as helping out at your child's school then imagine yourself in twenty years' time (if you want to be morbid, you can imagine yourself on your death bed). What will you regret not having done? What will you wish you had made time to do? What would you like to be remembered or known for? Will you wish you had spent more time Hoovering so that everyone reminisces about how clean you kept your floor? Or will it be something else?

Put writing time in your diary just like any other commitment and stick to it. Start small by blocking out just twenty minutes a day. If you can't manage that, then you may need to rethink how much you actually want to finish a book.

Now that you have located the time, now you have to protect that time with all the ferocity of a mother bear.

This can be hard. Believe me, I know. When my children were little, I used to use family holidays and weekends to grab a few hours of writing time because my husband/family were around to make sure my pre-schoolers didn't wander into traffic. The guilt, however, was immense.

I felt like a bad parent (and spouse) for abandoning my family in favour of my 'hobby'.

This is what I told myself, though (and, because I am the luckiest woman in the world, what my husband used to say, too): If writing is important to you then you owe it to your children to pursue it. You aren't just a parent, you are a role model and you are demonstrating that it is okay to put your own needs before others sometimes. You are demonstrating that you value creative pursuits and that you are willing and able to do hard, focused work in pursuit of your dreams.

If you are not a parent (or you don't struggle with parental guilt) you can substitute 'yourself' in the above for 'your children'. You owe it to yourself to take writing seriously and to give it the time it needs.

Nobody is going to respect your time if you don't. In other words, if you write in your diary that at ten o'clock until eleven on Saturday morning you are going to write and then you agree to go for coffee when your partner or friend invites you, you are simply telling them that your writing time isn't important.

Another technique (and feel free to ignore this if it isn't for you and you never intend to publish your work) is to stop calling your writing a 'hobby'. To yourself, at least.

While calling writing 'work' can be a double-edged sword (imbuing it with negative connotations of being hard and something we have to do, something we need a holiday from) there is no doubt that calling it 'work' can really help you to respect the time it takes. If you see the writing time as an investment (you are learning your craft that will eventually make money) it can ease the guilt and give you strength and motivation.

Scheduling

If you are anything like me, you will instinctively resist this tip. We are creative, free-flowing types. We may have accepted that we can't wait for the muse and have to write every day, but scheduling is a step too far. It just sounds so… Corporate. So business-like and sterile.

I get this reaction. Truly, I do. But, personally, I shake my fist at my younger self and curse the wasted weeks and months (and years) before I forced myself to embrace scheduling. I am so much more productive, now, and so much happier, too. I am far more likely to have proper time off (I just took a lunch break in which I sat at the dining table and read a book while I ate) and I feel more in control.

So. What exactly does it mean? If you are wincing at images of Excel spreadsheets, meetings with meaningless agendas, and the like, take a deep breath. It just means putting things in your diary on a specific day and time.

You already use scheduling in your life. If you have children, you write down their play dates and doctor's appointments, their tennis lessons and holiday dates. If you don't have children, I bet you write down (or tap into your calendar app) the day and time of your spin class and the dinner with your friends, you and your partner's dentist appointments and the week in France you have booked or music gig you have bought tickets for.

Unless you live the quiet life of a true hermit, you will have appointments and responsibilities, dates and days out, all of which get a note as to their date, time, and duration so that you don't end up double-booked or forget them entirely.

If you work (or parent) full-time you won't have many available times in which to write, so it might seem like overkill to schedule. After all, you can easily remember 'write for half an hour' every day. However, I would argue that it is powerful to give it a time slot. It's your life and if something comes up that means you wish to reschedule, you can, but there is a powerful difference between rescheduling an existing appointment versus 'just doing it later'. It also makes you less likely to skip if you know you will have to find a time later in your day (which you will schedule there and then) as opposed to a vague 'later'.

You are also signalling to your brain (and the others in your life) that this is important. By writing it down you are putting it on the same level as your other appointments which gives it status, while also reducing it to the manage-able and real. If writing is just as important (but no more important or strange) than going to the gym or meeting a friend then it will become a tiny bit less daunting too. You are bringing it into the everyday, the usual.

Something which helped me was to remember that my writing appointment was just that. An appointment to write. Yes, I usually have a daily word count I aim for, but the appointment to write is not an appointment to 'write 1000 words'. I am, instead, making a commitment to spend that time writing. If I tell myself that all I have to do is show up at the keyboard and focus on my book for thirty minutes or an hour and that even if I stare at a blank screen (or free-write about how stuck I am, producing zero usable words for the book) then it takes the pressure off. I have never once managed to spend more than five minutes staring at a blank screen. It's too boring. I either give in and get distracted (bad! Don't do that!) or, if I persevere with my distraction-free writing session, I start writing. Even if I start with a stream of consciousness ('I can't do this, it's too hard'), I eventually get something written.

The bottom line is that you are not making an appointment to write a certain number of good words, you are making an appointment to work on your craft. And that just means showing up, sitting down and not doing ANYTHING ELSE except writing/trying to write.

Note for those who write full-time

It is the dream for many of us but the transition from working full or part-time and writing in the edges of the day and writing full-time can be tricky.

It is a truism that tasks expand to fill the time available and that tight time constraints can focus the mind wonderfully. I know that when my youngest went to primary school and I suddenly, for the first time, had from 9.15 a.m. to 2.45 p.m. to myself I wrote no more words than when I had crammed my creativity into the two hours he had been at nursery.

Using a full day effectively did not come easily. It has been a long process of trying different methods, changing my mindset and improving my stamina and, I'll be honest, it is still an ongoing process of learning and practice. I still have days which seem to disappear with little to show for them but, thankfully, they are far rarer.

Those first longer days led to my peak procrastination years. I'm embarrassed to admit it, but there is a reason I used to refer to myself as the Queen of Procrastination and that reason included watching *Buffy The Vampire Slayer* and *The Gilmore Girls* for a 'little break' which stretched from eleven in the morning until school pick-up.

There is something about that whole day rolling out before you, seemingly acres of time, which leads to indecision, avoidance, laziness, and fear. The freedom is both intoxicating and paralysing and something I, over-confident from years of freelancing around full-time motherhood of babies and pre-schoolers, did not expect to have difficulty with.

And this is why I tell you this now. I didn't plan for it. I didn't expect to struggle with procrastination (I had the thing I had been looking forward to for ages – proper time in which to write!) so I didn't prepare.

When I think about my working days now (which are far longer – from 6.45 a.m. to around 5 p.m.) and how much I get done, how little time I spend faffing or wasting on the internet (there's still a bit, I admit; I'm not perfect!), I cannot believe the difference. I look back five years and it's like a whole different life.

Over time I made small changes with many steps backwards and then forward again. I have had to relearn these lessons over and over again and I fully expect to have to relearn them again in the future. We are all ongoing projects and, of course, life flings us curveballs which can knock our focus and routine.

Here are the key things I have found for cutting procrastination and forming good work habits:

1. Understand procrastination and ban the word 'lazy'
2. Schedule, schedule, schedule
3. Targets, goals, to-do lists, planning, and measuring

1. Understand Procrastination and ban the word 'lazy'

Being more understanding (and kind) to myself about my

own procrastination (rather than berating myself using negative language) was key. I had always favoured the stick method of motivation but by introducing the carrot (well, that sounds rude) and putting away the stick as much as possible, I felt better about myself and therefore stronger and my work became a more pleasant place to be, rather than a source of shame and misery over my continual under-achievement.

2.Schedule, schedule, schedule

When you have all day in which to write 1000 words and you know that can be done in one (good) hour, suddenly it doesn't seem that urgent. You know that the morning is your best time and that once it's done you can enjoy the rest of the day without it hanging over you. You know that if you do that, you will be able to take time off to do fun stuff and not feel guilty and you want to be a professional and Do The Work but, somehow, four o'clock rolls around and you still haven't opened the Word document, you are surrounded by biscuit crumbs and you have watched an entire season on Netflix.

If, however, you schedule your day (even a small amount) it will no longer be a seemingly endless stretch of empty time. For example: I walk every day at 11 a.m. It is scheduled as that means writing time before (morning is my best time creatively but, as I start before seven, I am ready for a break by that time) and lunch after (I tried going at 12 p.m. to make it part of a lunch break, but I was getting too hungry). After a few weeks of forcing myself to go out at this time, it became habit and I now instinctively start looking at the clock at that time, my body and mind ready. It is almost harder work not to go on my walk now, and I actually miss it when my routine is disrupted.

I'm not alone in using a timetable to get my work done. Stephanie Burgis explained to me that:

'It makes me very motivated. I have to get the work done. I can't sit there procrastinating... I have deadlines and a career I'd like to progress and so on and that's enough most days to push me past the initial inertia and reluctance... Having a very strict timetable and only a limited amount of time makes me very eager to begin my writing.'

Once you have practised putting one or two things on your schedule (and sticking to them) you will begin to view the things you write down in your diary for your writing as important as the other stuff. Then you can add in more.

Another example from my week is that 2–3 p.m. is podcast time. I schedule interviews, edit the audio, write questions, and research interviewees. 3–4 p.m. is marketing/admin/email for my author business. After 4 p.m. I tend to be fairly knackered (and my children come home from school) so this is when I do research and reading.

Even if you don't run a separate brand as I do with The Worried Writer, you should still schedule the different things you want to get done. Start with a proper start time and end time for your working day, including breaks. Morning break of twenty minutes, an hour at lunchtime, twenty minutes in the afternoon. Then add in things like reading time, meditation, exercise, and time to deal with your email. There. Already the day is no longer a mass of uncounted minutes.

Do the same with your week, writing in 'real life' appointments and holidays as well as writing deadlines so that you are no longer kidding yourself that you have week after week free and empty in which to procrastinate. Over time you can increase your use of scheduling but I promise that even a little will help.

Another – very pleasant – side-effect of scheduling is that I can now enjoy time off. Not just on holiday, but every day. I can reward a morning of good work with an hour of 'reading for fun' or 'faffing online' and truly enjoy it.

I used to spend my days with that horrible, 'I should be doing something else' feeling. Evenings and weekends were no different to weekdays and, from the moment I woke up until the moment I went to sleep I had the 'I ought to be doing my homework' feeling. I was a writer. I was always 'on', always working (or, supposed to be working). It made me feel like a writer and a true creative ('oh, yes, I'm always writing/thinking about writing') but the continual guilt, the constant nagging sense of underachievement was debili-tating and miserable.

These days, if I wake up with a cold or a headache, and the writing is going very slowly, I can be kind to myself. I can say 'you've worked really hard this week, you can cancel this afternoon's 2 p.m. podcast session and your 3 p.m. marketing session'. Then, with the prospect of treats ahead (and glow you get when your boss is super-nice to you), I instantly feel more able to tackle my writing session. I might not manage as much as usual (I am ill and feeble, don't forget!) but I manage something – which is more than I would have in my old way of doing things. And I get a lovely, guilt-free afternoon off, snuggled in bed with a book.

3. Targets, goals, to-do lists, planning, and measuring

Each of these things helped but combined (and I introduced them gradually – don't feel you need to start all of them at once) they stop me from lying to myself. I can still lose hours to procrastination or flailing but it is much harder to lose weeks. So I don't. When everything is planned and then performance is measured (word count, time spent writing, etc) and those metrics are looked at every day in a planner, on a wall chart, on a sticker chart, they are harder to ignore. The gaps are glaring and unpleasant and you start to avoid creating them.

Extra tip! Add stuff until you are busy enough

This works in conjunction with scheduling but may be a moot point for you. If you write full-time but have time-consuming personal responsibilities, health issues, or more deadlines than you can handle, then skip this tip. However, if you can relate to the following – the busier I am, the more I get done, then read on... I have found over the years that I have an optimum level of busy-ness. If I have too little going on, my energy and motivation slumps and I do less and less until I grind to a halt. This is partly because my worries expand to fill the space available and if I don't have enough to worry about a little, I end up worrying about the one or two things a lot.

Also, I find momentum keeps me powering on and to get a good amount of momentum I need to be busy. I find making decisions really difficult (really, really difficult) but once I have made one or two, it is easier for me to keep going.

Having lots on my plate makes my 'I must get on' panic set in which helps to get me started and stops me from spending too long on each individual task or decision. This energy will often carry from one thing to another, too, so if I do something scary (like writing fiction or sending an anxiety-inducing email) I get a little spark of energy that I can use to do something else. And so on.

Finally, having a variety of tasks on the go means that I

can pick and choose what I feel like doing, or have the mental energy for. As an example, when I'm not feeling creative these days (in between big projects) or have already used up my fiction brain for the day and got my words down, there are lots of things I can do; administration, marketing, podcast, non-fiction articles, research. Or I can switch projects and work on a different story idea or some learning.

There is, of course, a danger to adding things into the mix. Over-work, overwhelm, and stress can make me grind to a complete halt, so it's a delicate balancing act and one which shifts depending on my health and mood, as well as with external factors. Experiment in your own writing life to find your own optimum level of busy-ness. Don't be afraid to add things in (or to take them out again!) until you reach that pleasant, productive state.

9

REWIRE YOUR BRAIN ON TIME

As you may know, I answer questions from listeners on the podcast. Often, the same question is asked many times and one super-common one was typified in this message from Helen Redfern. Helen asked:

'How do I learn to write for just ten minutes? I feel that if I don't have a few hours uninterrupted there's no point in starting and just doing ten minutes. How do I change that?'

I definitely used to struggle with this, but I have managed to shift my thinking on it. I say 'shift my thinking' because that's really what is required. You have to alter your perspective on ten minutes so that you stop viewing it as a tiny, unusable slice of time.

First off, I suggest you prove yourself wrong:

Set a timer for ten minutes and write. Not to add wonderful words to your manuscript, but purely as an exercise. See how many words you have written when the timer goes off. It doesn't matter if you have thirty, fifty, or a hundred words, it is concrete evidence that *something* can be achieved in that time.

If you're feeling too much resistance to this idea and you really feel you cannot write for just ten minutes, do consider that this is fear talking. Fear is wily and flexible and, in this case, it is offering a reasonable-sounding excuse to prevent you from having to put words down.

The way to blast that excuse is to set the timer for ten minutes and NOT WRITE. You have to sit and stare at the blank screen or page of your notebook and not write a single word. You can't do anything else, either; no music to listen to, no browsing the internet, no reading. Just sit for ten minutes. I bet you'll be surprised at how long that actually is.

Okay, so once you've proved it's possible, you might still feel that it isn't worth it. That adding seventy-five words to your book or working for ten minutes is a drop in the ocean.

Now, you need to make it fun - make it into a challenge:

- See how many micro writing sessions you can fit in this week. Reward yourself for every ten minute session. I like stickers so I suggest you award a sticker for every ten minute session over a week. At the end of the week, count them up and marvel at the hours you have worked. Congratulate yourself on your wizardry – you have created writing time where none existed before!
- Draw a grid of boxes on a sheet of paper or use some squared paper. Every time you work on your book for ten minutes, colour in a box. When

you look at that ever-expanding block of colour you'll have a visual reminder of how that time adds up.

- Prepare for your ten minute sessions so that they are as valuable as possible. Make your tea or coffee before your allotted writing time, prepare your work space in advance.
- Prepare mentally, too: If you know you could grab some time when you get home from work, then use the commute to think about your story and characters and to get excited about what you'd like to write next.
- Every writer is different and if you discover that micro-sessions do not suit your process then feel free to swap 'thinking about my story' for 'writing' and see if that works instead. For example, when I'm rewriting I find it particularly hard to write in small chunks, but I can engage with my story and my characters or mull over a plot problem.

Finally, it's good to remember and to truly understand – deep in your bones – that this is how books are written.

They are written in small chunks. Word by word. Sentence by sentence. Paragraph by paragraph.

As hard as writing is, I think we sometimes think it ought to be even harder. So difficult that we couldn't possibly dash off a few sentences while waiting for the kettle to boil. The secret, if there is such a thing, is that the time taken to write the words does not reflect the quality of the writing. Some will come out well and some will not. Some will be cut and some will not. And, sometimes, words dashed off between appointments will be the very best, because you didn't have time to second-guess yourself and were able to access your muse or subconscious or wherever you believe your writing comes from directly.

A final tip is to consciously alter your thoughts. I know that mantras and affirmations sound a bit 'out there', but they do work. I like to use positive phrases which have success built-in. They describe the belief or behaviour as if I already possess it, making me feel instantly more positive and capable.

So, for this issue, I would use something like: 'I am the kind of person who grabs every spare moment and uses it to write.'

If this doesn't speak to you, try different wording until you find something which chimes. Then repeat it. Whenever you remember to do so and whenever you think about your writing or schedule. It will feel false and ridiculous, but if you stick with it you will find the statement becomes more plausible. Repeat it often enough and you will believe it. Magic!

10

SKIP PAST NEGATIVITY

Now that I have reached the ripe old age of forty, I have finally realised something. If you are not an inveterate people-pleaser like me, you may not need this lesson, but to all the rest of you - come close and I will whisper it in your ear... You do not owe anybody your attention.

I was brought up to be nice and I like to think of myself as a kind person, but this has meant that I have clocked a fair amount of time around people who are not good for me. By which I mean that their negativity or belittling attitudes or unkindness was allowed into my world way past the point when I should have moved on.

Thankfully, I am much stronger these days and it has also provided me with the perfect attitude for my writing world; I surround myself with positivity and move away from those who are negative as soon as possible.

When it comes to writing, especially for fragile, worrying, self-doubting writers (which includes most of us at least some of the time!), we need to be very careful about what external voices we allow into our world.

So, while I recommend finding a community of writers via forums, groups, courses and so on, it's vitally important that you find the right one. If it is a negative, bitter group of people, sniping at the world and complaining that the publishing industry doesn't know anything and that it's not fair that terrible writers make money and so on, then run away. Run away fast.

Using your own judgment (and following your gut instinct) is doubly important if you are going to be showing your work to a critique group. I was very lucky in the online group I found and it was filled with talented (and kind) people (most of whom have gone on to get agents and publishing contracts).

However, not all groups are created equal and there is a real danger of encountering bad critiques from the ill-informed or jealousy-fuelled, which could crush somebody starting out. It's important to learn to take constructive criticism and, if you decide to publish your work, you will need to handle and act upon editorial guidance, but you also need to develop your own instincts as a writer and your own voice/style. There is a danger of showing your work too soon and being derailed by a casual (or spiteful) comment. Always filter outside opinion according to who is giving it to you and weight them accordingly. For example, the thoughtful comments of your critique partner should be given more weight than those of a random person on a forum.

More importantly, though, is your own gut. Helpful editorial comments always chime somewhere deep within. You think 'oh, yes,' and 'why didn't I see that? How embarrassing.' Or they point out something which you knew wasn't quite right but were just hoping wasn't as bad as you thought. Or that you might get away with, somehow. If you don't agree with an editorial comment (regardless of the source) you can choose to ignore it. Ultimately, it is your book. Your writing. Yours.

Finding the line between protecting your vision and voice and taking criticism that will genuinely improve your book is something which definitely gets easier with experience. The only way is to keep going. Keep writing lots and your own voice will get stronger, your grasp of the craft will improve and you will also become more desensitised to the - often painful - business of discussing your work. In my early days, when a friend (or lecturer or my agent) began to talk about my book, I used to go hot and cold all over and physically shake, like I had the flu. Now, perhaps because the more you write the less attached to each piece you become (I'm attached while I'm writing, but by the time I get to the editorial process I'm starting to let go a little), this hardly ever happens. All of which is to say 'it gets easier'. I promise.

Protecting your work begins as soon as you decide to pursue writing. Even if you are not planning to show your work, I recommend you refrain from talking about your plans too much with your wider circle. Even well-meaning comments from friends and family can bruise your sense of purpose, derailing your writing for days or weeks at a time.

'Getting published is like winning the lottery.'

'Agents get thousands of submissions and only take on, like, two clients a year.'

'You'll never make any money doing that.'

'When are you going to get a proper job?'

Let me tell you a little story (don't worry, I'll keep it short!). When I was at university, I decided that I wanted to work in magazines. I knew that I wanted to be a writer but I was too scared to admit that what I really wanted to do was write books (and I was terrified that I wasn't talented or clever enough to even try). So, writing for magazines was my 'sensible' option. Of course, the rest of the world didn't react like that. I was told, repeatedly, that they were impossible to get into, that very few 'made it', and that I would have to live in London (which I didn't want to do).

If I had listened, I wouldn't have done work experience with a local magazine (so much fun!) which led to my first paying freelance gig for a national style magazine. When I graduated, I found a big publishing house outside of London (bonus - it was in the beautiful city of Bath) and I did two weeks of work experience. I couldn't work for free for any longer than that (rent to pay!), but it didn't matter as I had made contacts who let me know there was a job opening for editorial assistant on Computer Arts magazine. I had an interview and got the job. That's not the kind of story that's going to make an inspirational film and I'm not claiming to be a massive success story in the world of media, but I did have a wonderful job which I thoroughly enjoyed, working with brilliant, enthusiastic people. And when I left to have my daughter, I worked freelance, writing for lots of different magazines using the experience and contacts I'd gathered. None of which would have happened if I had let the naysayers stop me from even trying.

So, be careful to whom you reveal your writing ambitions, and remember that you don't have any obligation to tell people, even if they ask.

Having said all that, I do think support is important, so do tell trusted people who will support you and cheer you on.

Later on, when you have 'come out' as a writer or it is common knowledge because your books are now for sale, do remember that casual comments from people who are not writers are, essentially, nonsense. Not to be rude (there is no reason for them to know the realities of the modern publishing world, after all) but when people ask you if you are 'rich now' or 'when is the film coming out?' or 'why don't you write a children's book like that clever J.K. Rowling?' you have to not be annoyed or take it personally. They are (probably) not meaning to make you feel judged or criticised and are just making small talk. As they are not inside your head, they have no idea how potentially crushing these kinds of 'advice' can be.

Personally, I've been very lucky and have been bowled over by the supportive comments I've had from people or even, which is surreal and gratifying, how impressed friends and acquaintances have been that I have written books (let alone had them published). However, I have heard enough horror stories from my writer friends to know that this is not always the case and, if necessary, you must develop selective hearing loss.

There are, unfortunately, exceptions to the above. There might be a person in your life who isn't making innocent comments but deliberately undermining you and your dreams. If this is the case then you should definitely avoid discussing your writing or ambitions with them. It is also worth noting that they are not being a good friend, and you might consider spending less of your valuable time with them.

Avoiding Negativity After Publication

One of the hardest things about achieving your dream of becoming a published author (cue the world's smallest violin!) is that it doesn't change your life. Or, more accurately, it might change aspects of your life but it doesn't change you.

Having been so lacking in self-confidence and so

desperate for the industry seal of approval an agent and a publishing contract would give, it was a hard blow when I woke up fundamentally the same person. Yes, I was thrilled beyond belief. Yes, it was brilliant to be able to tell the people who had been supporting me for years 'I did it!'. But the worries and insecurities did not disappear. Some of them retreated a little, while others grew. And the worry of 'will I ever get a publishing contract' was immediately replaced with the worry of 'will I be able to write another publishable book?'. With the added pressure of a deadline.

Essentially I had swapped one set of problems for new ones.

Here follows my advice for surviving and thriving post-publication.

Don't read reviews

Yes, I hereby give you permission not to read your reviews. I felt guilty about this initially as it felt disrespectful to the readers but, very quickly, I realised that good reviews gave me a moment of pleasure, but bad ones knocked me out for days and that I wasn't going to be able to produce books for my beloved readers if I was rocking in a corner unable to write.

Maybe you are tougher than me, and more power to you, but I don't believe we have an obligation to read everything written about us on the internet.

My exception to this is book blogs. I greatly value book bloggers and the wonderful work they do and I do tend to read those as I know how much time and thought they put into their work. In fairness, though, I have been very lucky and I haven't had a truly negative review from a blogger. If that starts to happen, I will probably re-think my policy!

As I said, I felt guilty for not reading the reviews on

Amazon, Kobo and iBooks and, naturally, my curiosity about them didn't just disappear the moment I realised it was doing me more harm than good to pour over them. However, I have a system which I highly recommend. My husband reads my reviews and tells me when I have a particularly good one. He also regularly emails me with little bursts of 'motivation' - a few lines from a particularly nice review or some news like 'another three five star reviews on Amazon!'. This way, I feel as if they are being noted and respected, but without risk to my own fragile psyche.

When I interviewed bestselling author Annie Lyons, I found that her friend went one step further:

> 'My best friend made me this [points to poster on wall], for my fortieth birthday, 'forty fabulous reviews for a fabulous forty year old'. She did this beautiful thing and designed it all... It's a beautiful thing and it's nice to have something like that in your writing room or writing space.'

Similar to my suggestion for pre-published writers about gathering positive comments and encouragement into one place, to look at during the bad times, I think gathering some really good reviews or comments from your editor or agent and putting them into a document/scrapbook and looking at it regularly is a good idea.

Know your own triggers

Identify the kinds of things which are likely to make you feel inferior or negative and avoid them. If you are having a bad day and other people's good news on social media is making you feel like an underachieving loser, recognise that feeling and shut down your browser. Watch out for patterns in your own confidence and take note of what knocks you (and what builds you up).

For a while, my lifelong love of bookshops was spoiled as I felt insecure and envious of the books displayed there. I wanted, so desperately, to be able to find my own book on the shelf and to feel like a 'real' writer. For a short time they underlined not what I had achieved (publishing contracts!) but what I hadn't (a place on the 'three for two' table at the front of the shop). I knew it wasn't logical and that many people would love to have what I had, but the guilt only made me feel even worse (unsuccessful *and* a terrible person - double whammy!).

So I avoided bookshops. There is no rule which says you have to keep putting your hand in the flames!

Now that I am more comfortable with my own definition of success (a big hat tip to Joanna Penn of The Creative Penn for this), I can enjoy bookshops again (hooray!) so I'm certainly not suggesting that you will have to avoid those triggers forever; just when you are feeling especially sensitive.

My definition of success (and yours may well be different) is making a living with my writing, which I equate to earning at least as much as I would in an averagely-paid job, having lots of happy readers, making a difference to other writers and supporting the writing community, and creating work I am proud of while being authentic.

My publishing contract with Lake Union might not have got me into the high street bookshops but the editors I worked with were amazing (and I am proud of the book) and, not to be too vulgar, I make decent money from the deal. Best of all, I get regular messages from readers telling me how much they enjoyed it. In other words, it hits my definition of success and makes me very happy. It's good to strive for things, of course, but defining your own success helps you to recognise your achievements when they happen and puts the locus of control firmly into your own hands.

It also helps with one of the biggest barriers to positivity in your working life - comparing your own progress with others. Trust me when I say, this way misery lies and the very best thing you can do for your writing life is to keep your eyes on your own work.

Stop comparing yourself to other writers

First off, and this is something I learned in life which definitely applies to writing; you can't compare your insides with other people's outsides. What do I mean by that? In life, you can't compare the way you feel inside (crap and tired, for example) with the way other people appear on the outside (smiling, perfectly-coiffed, and with a sparkling clean house and a job with a high salary). You do not know how they feel inside so you are comparing two different things. Maybe they are also tired. Maybe they have both a perfect house and a perfect job because they hire help? Maybe they don't hire help but they are miserable with the stress of maintaining the standards they have set. Maybe they hate their high-paying job. None of which is to wish misery on another person but just to point out that you, looking from the outside, simply do not know the whole story.

Now, apply this thinking to your writing jealousies and insecurities.

We all work in a ridiculously difficult and fickle industry. We ply our trade, spinning stories for others and hoping that they enjoy them. We bare our souls and hope to get financial remuneration in return. Make no mistake, it is not a psychologically-easy pastime, and all of us will struggle at some point.

Given that, when you next read about somebody's mega-deal and feel that stab of envy, remind yourself that writer is a person just like you. They struggled with that manuscript and worried about whether they were good enough, whether the story was any good. They put their heart and soul into it, just as you do with your own work.

Next, remember that this is a long game. You don't know what that particular writer went through before getting that deal (even if they are lauded as a debut success, the chances are that is not the first book they have written!) and you don't know what will happen next for them. I have thought about the pressures which come with big deals and, having felt a lot of pressure with even modest publishing contracts, I have since realised that I was lucky not to land some massive, high-profile deal with my first book.

There are plenty of people who succumb to the dreaded 'second book syndrome' and I definitely found writing the follow-up to my debut incredibly stressful and difficult. I can only imagine how much harder that would have been if I had been given a massive advance or had achieved a level of fame or wide acclaim with my first foray.

In a related note, remember that this is a long game for you, too. Just because your debut didn't set the world on fire, doesn't mean your third or fifth book won't. Chocolat is probably Joanne Harris's best-known book (thanks to the film adaptation starring Juliette Binoche and Johnny Depp) but it was her third published novel.

It's also too soon to say what has been a success and what has not. Both in the sense that only history will decide on what work was 'important' or 'great' (just think of the writers and artists who were marginalised or considered low brow in their time and have gone on to be considered classic fifty years later) and in the more immediate sense of our own careers. Digital books mean that we no longer go out of print. Books can (and do) sell steadily over time making a novel which had a modest launch a success over five years. Books can be discovered at any time so your debut may get picked up by a film producer or awards body in ten years' time and given a whole new lease of life.

I don't know about you, but I want a long career doing this. I want to earn a living and I want to keep on writing and publishing and I want, at the end of my career, to look back on a shelf full of books I am proud of. I want to be able to say that I improved my craft and that I put my heart and soul into the stories and worked on them to the best of my abilities. Your aims and ambitions might be different and that's completely fine, but I urge you to spend some time thinking about those aims and the things which are important to you. It's easier to measure your own worth and success against your own progress, when you know exactly what your own metrics for this are.

I do recommend taking a long-term view for another key reason; when you focus on your (hopefully) long life as a writer, you become less concerned with the success or progress of each individual book. Yes, I'm still obsessed with the story I am currently working on (such is the nature of novel-writing) but I am far less obsessed with the external success of each.

Scarcity versus abundance

As always, attitude is everything.

There are people who greet each new technological development with a sigh, saying 'even fewer people will read' and each new bestselling author with the feeling that another 'spot' has been taken. They focus on news stories about declining book sales (or book shops or rates of teenagers reading) and see every other writer as a competitor.

They are operating with an attitude of scarcity; the belief that there are only a small amount of resources (readers) to go around and every time somebody publishes a book it is taking away from their personal potential number of customers.

You know, I feel miserable just typing all that.

There are others - myself included - who prefer to believe that we live in a time of abundance. People are reading more than ever before (textual communication, social media, books on cheap smart phones, e-readers bringing affordability and convenience). Yes, as writers we are competing for people's time with games, films and television, but, as creatives, we also benefit from the amazing quality of story-telling that is available in those media. Plus, there are opportunities in script-writing and game-narratives.

I choose to see my fellow authors as colleagues, not competitors. Every time a book becomes a bestseller and races up the charts, it is a triumph for all books, a success for reading. And happy readers don't read one book and then stop, they pick up another and another. Every time there is a break-out, nobody-saw-that-coming success such as Fifty Shades of Grey or Harry Potter, I think of all the reluctant or non-readers who were inspired to pick up that book. And how much joy they now have from a newly-discovered love of reading. Plus, from a business point of view, all those other books they may pick up in the future...

But what about the number of books being published? What about self-publishing opening the floodgates and saturating the market?

Two things: First, all writers are readers so more people publishing equals more books being sold/read.

And secondly, just because things are technically available for sale does not mean they will sell. Only good stories, properly marketed (with decent covers etc) will find their readership. That is the same whether they are put out by a publisher or the author.

I prefer to focus on the fact that it is a golden time for writers and readers. Twenty years ago, a writer whose books appealed to a small niche in the market would either never reach those readers (as a publisher would not take the chance) or they would not be able to sustain a career. Now, with the ability to find your own readers and sell directly to them, writers can find their tribe and make enough money to pay some bills.

For readers who like books other than the mainstream, this means they can find exactly what they like to read. And, quite possibly, enjoy a closer relationship with the creator. Similar to the way in which indie musicians have long been able to build a small, but loyal, fanbase by circumventing the record companies, writers now have the same opportunity. For more on this ethos, I highly recommend Amanda Palmer's book *The Art of Asking*, as well as Joanna Penn's *Business For Authors*.

Ultimately, you create your own experience of reality by the things you choose to give attention, the people you surround yourself with, and the thoughts you dwell upon. Positive thinking is not an instant fix and I'm not, of course, suggesting that those who are suffering with pain or illness, real poverty or danger can change their circumstances with a happy thought or two, but for those of us lucky enough to live in the top five per cent of wealthy people (with our basic needs fulfilled on a daily basis), making the choice to be positive and grateful is the only logical course.

Key Points:

- Define what success means TO YOU. When we chatted, Joanna Penn said:

'One level of success is winning a literary prize and having critics say how brilliant you are and the other one is selling multi-million books to readers and I decided at that point that my definition of success was to sell millions of books to readers... I would rather have Dan Brown's success than win the Booker Prize!'

- Keep your eyes on your own work!
- Don't discuss writing or publishing with negative people
- Learn (and avoid!) your own self-doubt triggers

11

IT TAKES A VILLAGE

They used to say it takes a village to raise a child and I say it takes a village to raise a writer. Although generally a solitary pursuit, writing doesn't have to be a lonely one. You *can* do it entirely on your own, of course, but if you are a worried writer, I recommend that you don't try.

Find your community

For all its faults, this is something the internet truly excels at – connecting like-minded people with shared passions.

When I decided to start writing (rather than dreaming about writing, writing endless entries in my journal about how I wasn't writing), I joined an online community of writers called WriteWords. It had a small subscription cost (which meant that it was populated with people who were serious about improving their writing and getting published) and it had lively forums and small critique groups dedicated to different forms and genres of writing. The people I met in the 'chick lit' group are still my friends today and most of us have gone on to get agents and publishing contracts. When people ask how I became friends with so many successful authors, the answer is usually that I met them back in the day when we were all 'aspiring' unpublished newbies.

Another place I built my community of writers is by reading blogs regularly (some would say obsessively). Over time, I began commenting and then having conversations. Some moved to Twitter where the chat became more regular and some morphed, over time, into regular emails and genuine friendships.

These days, as you are no doubt aware, Facebook is a treasure trove of specialist-interest groups. Search the site, join a few, and then spend some time reading posts and replies and getting a feel for the community. Is it your kind of place? If so, dive in and start making friends. It not, no worries, move on. Your perfect group is out there.

Another place I met like-minded people are courses, both in the 'real world' (my masters in Creative Writing) and online. As they are an investment of time and money, you tend to get a certain level of dedication and involvement from the participants and you may be able to find a critique or accountability partner. If you have chosen wisely, then you are also going to learn lots from the course content and teacher, too, which takes the pressure off the community-building aspect.

A quick word of warning! There are lots of online courses and workshops these days, many of which are wonderful and well-worth the fees charged. There are, however, lots of scammy, amateur, or just plain bad courses. Do your due diligence and research the course and tutor before parting with any cash.

Before we go any further, a quick digression on university degrees for creative writing. I say this as a person with a Masters (post-graduate degree) in Creative Writing (and as a person who loves and believes in education): There are many excellent reasons to do a degree in Creative Writing but 'getting published' is not one of them. Neither, I would say, is 'finishing your book'.

I had lots of (other) reasons for doing my post-grad and, as a result, am glad I did it, but the fact remains that I could have got better writing instruction (certainly more suited to my own voice/genre-preferences and career ambitions) by putting together my own education via books, online courses, workshops, and podcasts. In fact, I did. I would also add that the very best way to learn how to write a book is to write a book. And then another. And another. Learning as you go along.

Also, the atmosphere of academia is very rarefied and leans (often exclusively) towards literary fiction. Now, I knew this would be the case (I had an undergraduate degree in English Literature and had spoken to other post-grad students before signing up) but it was still slightly shocking how 'old school' the attitudes were. Not just to genre fiction or, pause for shocked intake of breath, *the desire to write commercial fiction*, but the lack of knowledge (or practical advice) for the students on making a living with their writing. There was one path and one path only; write a great literary masterpiece, get an agent and publisher, and then either win every prize available, or do another job to pay the bills while suffering elegantly in one's garret.

So, back to finding your tribe. Once you have found the forums, blogs or groups you like and have observed for a little while – join in! I know it's scary – trust me, I spent years lurking on blogs and forums, too shy to write a comment, but force yourself to interact as it really is the way to get the most from these places. Just be yourself (your 'best self', at any rate). Be polite. Be helpful. Be genuinely friendly, just as you would in your personal or 'real' life and you will make genuine connections. Over time, you will find that your cohort moves on together, learning and growing and gaining experience. Some people will stop writing (or pursuing publication) and some will race ahead, but you will form a core group you can rely on for support, advice, and encouragement.

I can honestly say that the writing friends I have made are absolutely vital to my continuing productivity and happiness. Nobody understands writing (and the heart-breaking/crazy/uncertain world of publishing) like other writers and nobody else (except your spouse if you are exceptionally lucky) will happily discuss plot problems, character arcs, and POV headaches for hours on end.

Mentors

In addition to finding your cohort of fellow writers, people who are at a similar place in their writing as you, I highly recommend you find yourself a mentor (or three!). I don't mean a person with whom you (necessarily) have a real-life mentoring contract, but a 'virtual mentor'; somebody you admire and learn from. While mentoring traditionally indicates a one-to-one relationship, but you can adopt a 'virtual mentor' by buying their books, attending their webinars or courses, listening to their podcasts, reading their articles, or otherwise following their work.

My virtual mentor, as I have stated several times on my podcast, is Joanna Penn of The Creative Penn. The Creative Penn is a brilliant podcast and website, which provides information and inspiration to self-publishing writers. Joanna also writes thrillers under the name J.F.Penn and has a range of non-fiction titles on topics such as business, creativity, and marketing. I began following Joanna over three years ago and she has made a huge difference to my writing life. When Joanna came onto my own podcast as a guest, I spent the first ten minutes wittering on and on (thankfully, off-air) in full fangirl-mode. I was completely starstruck but also felt as if I knew her; after all, I had spent hours listening to her voice and reading her words. I trust Joanna and her advice and I gain confidence and inspiration from following her; without her guidance and example, you would not be reading this book right now!

A word of advice when choosing your mentors: this might seem obvious, but look to people who live the life you want to live, not just people who have one or two external trappings of success which you find attractive. As always, your writing life is also your *life* life. Think about what is important to you and make sure you are choosing mentors who reflect your core values and ambitions.

12

BEAT THE BLOCK

There comes a time in every project when it gets hard. I mean, really hard. Writing a book is tricky, of course; there are many decisions to make, distractions at hand, and fears which rise up from the murky subconscious. I'm not talking about an ordinary 'tricky session', though, I'm talking about The Wall.

Some writers know exactly when they are going to hit The Wall because it happens at the same place every time. For some it's at the start with that clean white page. For others, it's a third of the way through or at the halfway mark, when you have run out of the excitement which kick-started the project but are still depressingly far from the end. Sometimes, the really hard bit is the last couple of chapters as you battle the fear of finishing. Finishing, after all, means letting go of the story, and having to send the manuscript to your agent or beta reader.

For me, things get tricky around 25--30,000 words and again at the halfway mark. Once I've got at least 60,000 words I know I've got enough 'stuff' to fill a book and that I'm going to finish it. I've abandoned a few at the 50,000 word mark, though, when I've hit The Wall hard.

I mention my failures for two reasons: Firstly, so that you know it's normal to fail. Writing is a continual process of failing and the quicker you get comfortable with that reality, the easier, happier, and more productive you will be!

Secondly, because sometimes it is okay to stop working on a book. Yes, finishing what you start is an essential skill and one you must develop, it is also true that some pieces of writing won't become finished novels. And that is okay. Maybe people who outline extensively don't have this problem (perhaps they discover the problems or abandon the project at that stage, instead) but it is possible to get to 30,000 or 50,000 words and realise that it's irrevocably, irretrievably wrong. Or that you don't like your main character. Or that you don't love the idea enough to go through the work necessary.

I bring up this possibility as when you are truly blocked, and The Wall seems insurmountable, there is a (very small) chance that your subconscious is trying to let you know that *this is the wrong book* to be working on. Maybe for right now, maybe forever. And if you accept that you are flogging a dead horse (horrible phrase, sorry) and put the manuscript on the shelf, you will regain your writing mojo with another project.

The difficulty, of course, lies in working out whether you have a normal block (halfway through/run out of steam/it's just too hard) or whether it is a sign you should give up on that particular book idea. Experience helps so that you are better able to read and trust your own writerly instincts. And, if nothing else, going through the following suggestion to beat the block, should help you to clarify matters. I won't pretend, though; it's one of the trickiest things about writing novels.

The only bit of silver-lining I can add is that nothing is wasted. Even if you do realise you need to shelve 50,000 words of manuscript, that is 50,000 words of practice. Every single one making you a better writer. Plus, you might be able to use characters, scenes, or plot ideas in another story later on. Or, and this has definitely happened to me, it's just not quite ready to be written. You might find that an abandoned book will benefit from being left to cook in the stove of your subconscious for a few months (or years), and you will be able to come back and finish it at a later date.

So, back to your manuscript and your block. First off, accept that writing a book is hard and it is perfectly acceptable to have bad days or weeks. Take that guilt or that feeling of 'not being a proper writer' and shove it firmly to one side.

How To Break Through The Wall

Ignore the advice above and tell yourself it's easy and fun

If you can manage this without loading yourself with guilt or pressure, try reminding yourself that you are just telling a story. One way to do this is to write what you have so far in an omniscient manner. Start with 'Once upon a time...' as if you are telling yourself a bedtime story.

Reignite your passion

When you started this book you were excited (hopefully) and you just need to remember why. Write a list of all the stuff you think is cool in your story. I know I'm forty and not allowed to use the word 'cool' but in this instance it means the stuff that sets your brain on fire, the stuff that gives you that little shiver, that makes part of your soul whisper 'yes'.

This works if you are finding it difficult to get started on a project, too. Even though I compose almost exclusively using a computer, I like to have a new notebook for each new book. I doodle, paste pictures, and write notes and, at the beginning, I make a long list of all the feelings, ideas, and objects which are flying around my mind when I think of the new book. Here's an extract from the list from the note-book of the book which became *In The Light of What We See*:

- A very bad doctor.
- 1930s nurses standing around an operating table. The lights go out.
- Enamel bluebird brooch. (I pasted a picture of this in).
- Mina
- Ghost birds
- Long black hair in a braid tied with a white ribbon.

It doesn't matter if all of these things end up in the finished book, they are a jumping-off place and something you can read over at blocked times to remind yourself of the excitement and why you wanted to write this story in the first place.

You can also use this technique if you are struggling to find a story idea to start with. For those who meet The Wall when they attempt to think of a book idea, try making a list of everything you like when reading or watching fiction – everything, in short, you think is cool! For example, mine might begin:

- Swishy cloaks

- Telekinesis
- Old cinemas
- Peacock feathers

Don't censor yourself or think that you have to be clever or worthy or cool by anybody else's standards. This is just between you and your notebook.

Once you have your list, you might find you are already feeling the tug of an idea. If not, go through the list and pick out a couple of things and challenge yourself to fit them into a short story or vignette (using them as a very free and easy writing prompt).

Perhaps there is something on your list which you would like to know more about. Allow yourself to follow that impulse of curiosity with research and reading, making notes along the way. Ask yourself 'what if?' questions and 'why?' and 'how?'.

Recognise self-censorship and fear of judgement

I don't know if you can relate to this experience, but sometimes when I am writing I get an actual, physical sensation of embarrassment. I find myself toning down the dialogue of a character or the action in a scene or pulling back from a particular storyline. Sometimes, this feeling of fear and embarrassment actually stops me from writing a scene altogether, so I thought it was worth mentioning in this 'block' section.

All I want to say is that you are not alone and, having discussed it with many authors, I know that this feeling is completely normal. When I interviewed bestselling psychological thriller author Mark Edwards, he described his own experience of self-censorship:

'I suppose there is part of me when I'm writing that thinks, "Oh my God, what's my mum going to think about this?"

In fact, if I find my inner censor screaming at me I often think that means it's a powerful scene and I should keep it in.'

I completely agree with Mark. Usually the places where I feel most uncomfortable (that I am being too dark or too emotional or I feel 'exposed') result in the writing that really connects with readers.

Stuck on a particular scene or don't know where the story goes next?

Perhaps your block is more practical in nature. You aren't questioning your desire to write the story, just your ability to get past the place in which you are stuck…

Skip ahead. I often do this. I put a placeholder in the place I'm stuck using // marks so that I can find it easily when editing. A note might look like this:

//They argue here and something is revealed//

Or

//No idea what happens here//

Or

//Make this better//

Yes, often I curse 'past Sarah' when I come back to these unhelpful notes, but sometimes everything I've written since tells me exactly what needs to happen in the place I was stuck.

Or that I don't need the scene after all and can simply cut it.

Play with POV

Another way to approach a sticky scene is to switch point of view. Just as a writing exercise (not for the final version of the book), try switching from first to third (or vice versa) and see if it shakes something loose. Or, you can describe the scene from another character's point of view. Again, this is just an exercise, not intended to be included in the manuscript, so there is no pressure and you might be surprised about what you discover.

Take a run-up at it. Something I often do when stuck with a 'what on earth happens next?' question is to put myself in each of my main character's shoes. I free-write from their point of view (in first person, regardless of how the actual narrative is written) and just talk to 'myself' about everything that has happened and how 'I' feel about it. More often than not, this tells me what my character would do next.

This is good for the emotions and character arcs, too. If you are finding it hard to connect with a character or don't feel that you know them well enough.

If you are writing a thriller or mystery, you can also try this from the antagonist's point of view. Even if you never actually see this point of view in your actual book, spending some time in their head can help you to develop a more well-rounded character, as well as working out what needs to happen next in the story.

Take a 'high level' approach to character

Speaking of the antagonist, this is another great way to overcome a block. Think about your story in terms of archetypes. Take a step back and look at the function that each of your characters is performing. You have your protagonist (the hero or heroine), the antagonist (the baddie), and their conflicting goals.

Change of scenery

Another technique is to take yourself away from the screen. Switch things up by writing longhand in a notebook or speak into a voice recorder. Try doodling with different coloured pens on a big sheet of paper or making a mind-map of your story.

Go for a walk and let your mind mull over the problem while you get some fresh air. Other activities which occupy your brain and body but still leave space for thinking, such as housework, taking a shower, or knitting, can also be worth a try.

I spoke to Julie Cohen about using craft and exercise as part of her creative process:

> 'Knitting does help because it's repetitive. I don't think about my writing but it does kind of reset you... What really helps for writing is running. Walking as well... Something about the repetitive nature gets me thinking... It clears my mind *and* gives me ideas.'

There are so many different ways to approach your novel and some of these will work on one day and not on another. The thing to remember is that there is no perfect technique (although you will have your own favourites) and that you have lots of different techniques to try. If you keep at it, working on these things during your daily writing time, you will break through and make progress – I promise. The way to overcome a difficult bit or a block is to keep writing. To keep trying and thinking and staying engaged with your story. Ninety-nine per cent of the time this is the answer. The only way out is through. The only way to solve a writing problem is by writing.

When You Can't Even Begin

What if you want to write a book but you don't have any ideas?

Develop an idea-gathering habit by noticing what you are interested in. As Mark McGuinness said in his interview: 'Follow your curiosity.'.

Or, go a step further and take notes every day, training your brain to notice interesting things and filling up your sub-conscious with creative prompts. Joanna Penn went into detail on this when we spoke:

> 'I have an app on my phone called Things and I use Moleskine notebooks and I have a folder called "fiction ideas", and as I go about life I just write stuff in that folder. I was just watching a documentary about the ocean and they said something about shark skin which I just wrote down... Anything that I hear or see or experience I will write down in my folder and what I find is that things just bubble up from my sub-conscious... Keep the in-flow working so that the out-flow works as well.
>
> Maybe start off by writing one thing a day that you notice in the environment. And it needs to be really specific. One of the tips in fiction is that specific is much, much better, so it's not a blue flower, it's a blue iris in front of a Victorian terrace with the sun on the sunflower with a bee.'

What if you finish a book and you can't start a new one?

Sometimes we get blocked in between projects and can't even begin. This can be frightening ('I've lost it! I'll never write another book!') and, as always, the fear and anxiety don't help matters…

When you feel empty of ideas and the voices in your head have gone quiet it might be part of the natural cycle of creativity and rest. If you can't explain your malaise through non-writing problems (illness, a stressful life event) then it's possible that you are in a fallow period creatively -speaking and this isn't a cause for concern.

Something I have realised over the last ten years of writing is that after finishing a novel I am spent. I have given it my all and I feel utterly blank. In the past I used to panic about this, but now I plan for it and embrace it when it happens. It's a good sign – it means I worked hard and poured all of my creative energy into the last book and that's a very good thing!

While your creativity is endlessly renewable and will never run out in the larger, permanent sense, it is dished up in medium-sized scoops. Imagine a delicious pudding – a bowl of ice cream with sprinkles and sauce, perhaps. That's your creative energy and all the 'stuff' you are currently inspired by. As you write your book, you take spoonfuls of that ice cream. Every time you write a book you should keep on going until you are scraping the bowl with your metaphorical spoon. Go all out, hold nothing back. Just as you wouldn't keep a dribble of melted ice cream back for your next summer holiday, you don't want to keep anything in reserve when working on your current book. Use it all.

Then, when you finish and your pudding bowl is utterly empty, you need to rest and to refill that bowl before you can dive into a new project.

How to refill the bowl? Take some time off from writing and then, literally, refill the bowl. Not with ice cream (although I prescribe some of that, too – you just wrote a book for goodness' sake!) but with other literature and art.

The stuff that we consume is how we refuel both in creative and physical energy. So, just as you might eat real ice cream for the calorific energy, you need to consume great books, television, and films, visit art galleries or interesting places, go for walks in nature, try a new skill in an evening class or spend time with friends and family, to refill your bowl of creative energy.

If your schedule (or temperament) doesn't allow for a complete writing break, then you could try switching projects. I like to do lots of non-fiction writing (blog posts and articles, this book, personal stuff in my journal) in between novels but you could try switching genres or forms (screenplays, poetry, short stories), if that floats your boat.

The main thing is to refill with inspiration, though. Creative work is not made in a vacuum and every piece of work is inspired by the things we have experienced and seen, the other stories we have read. Don't worry about that – just trust that as soon as you fill your bowl with delicious ice cream, you will be ready to write again.

13

BAD WRITING DAYS

This chapter appeared originally on the Worried Writer site and I have reproduced it here un-changed as it represents a 'bad writing day' and the way I felt. I also felt extremely frightened about publishing this on the site – and almost didn't – but I had such a wonderful and supportive response from readers that it made me truly grateful that I had pushed my fear to one side and allowed myself to be vulnerable in public.

Bad Writing Days. We all have them.

We don't like to talk about them. We're frightened that by talking about them we will make them stronger. Or, worse still, we will jinx our productivity and conjure them into existence. No writer wants to say the word 'block'.

I've always struggled to write. There are two people inhabiting this body; one wants to be left alone to write, wants nothing more than acres of time in which to type and think and come up with sentences and words and passages of description and dialogue. The other one, unfortunately, wants to do anything else. Anything!

Both of these people, however, like *having written*.

There is a passage in Brené Brown's excellent book, *Rising Strong*, which explains that we must choose comfort or courage.

The toddler part of me bawled 'why can't I have both?', while the adult part of me nodded sagely, letting the words sink in and the truth trickle through…

I can't have both.

It's supposed to be scary.

I need to choose courage because that's where creation lies.

But on a bad writing day, I choose comfort over and over again. I choose to write this blog rather than open my work-in-progress because however frightening a personal post like this feels, it is nothing to the anxiety I feel about working on my book.

On a bad writing day, I choose to say 'yes' to a friend's invitation, even though I know it's during my writing time. I may pretend this is something else (the selfless act of a good friend, for example) but I am lying.

On a bad writing day, I slip into the comfortable routine of editing a piece of old work when I should be making something new. Or I take all day to write a paragraph, telling myself it's 'difficult' when the truth is, I am stalling.

On a bad writing day, I let the voices that tell me I'm worthless and my story is stupid and that I have no talent or creativity win.

I've had a lot of bad writing days recently. I've chosen comfort so often it's beginning to feel like my new routine.

Luckily, that frightens me. I see my life stretching ahead, filled with comfortable no-writing-days, and I imagine all the books I will never write, the stories I will never tell.

That frightens me enough to make me open my document and get back to work. I want to have written and I know fine well there's only one way for that to happen: courage.

14

ON NOT WRITING

Just a brief pause in the pom pom waving... I want to say a quick word about not writing.

Sometimes, life knocks you off your game. That is a fact and to pretend otherwise is disingenuous and, I think, unhelpful. Bereavement, divorce, illness, moving house, family problems, or issues in the wider world such as political instability can all push us from the path of productivity.

If this happens to you, please don't compound the problem with guilt and recriminations. The maxim 'writers write' is a handy reminder for days when you just don't really feel like it or are stuck in your plot, but in times of true stress, pain, or misery, it is like trying to put a plaster on a broken leg.

The truth of the matter is this: writing is not digging ditches. You can force yourself to turn up to the computer and you can even force your fingers to tap the keys, but if your brain (your subconscious, your soul) isn't capable, then you won't be able to write. It's important to recognise this and to fully accept that you are not a bad writer or a lazy person; sometimes your psyche will not be able to manage the deep creative work of writing and that is *not your fault*.

Oddly, by accepting that you absolutely cannot do it right now, you might find that you actually want to – a little bit. Once you have taken away the pressure of 'should' you might find that writing becomes your escape from the bad life situation and you might begin again.

Or, it might not and that is okay, too. This is not a productivity trick.

So, the first thing to remember is compassion. Have compassion and empathy for yourself and accept that writing is not an option for you at this time. I spoke about this with Stephanie Burgis and she agreed:

> 'Sometimes you can't. People go through terrible situations, people are overwhelmed... All those silly statements you'll see people making like 'real writers write' and 'real writers don't let anything stop them' are completely false.'

The second thing is to remind yourself that this is short-term. Yes, it might be months (or even years) before the situation improves and your writing brain wanders back from the wilderness, but it is time-bound. There will be a time when things are better and when you feel better. If your brain tells you that you have 'lost it' or that you will always feel this empty, it is lying to you. You feel that way because you are frightened and because you are unhappy and stressed. They are feelings, not facts.

What is a fact is that your writing will wait for you. You cannot 'lose it' as it is part of you. It is you. One of the most wonderful things about creative writing is that it is a very forgiving master. If you wish to be a world-class athlete there is an expiry date on your dream, but if you wish to write wonderful stories to entertain or illuminate it is never too late to start (or to start again).

Being kind to yourself and as accepting of the situation

as you can manage will go a long way to easing the stress of not writing.

Next is to keep an eye out for the returning creativity. Don't jump on the first inkling of an idea with a 'that's it, I'm back, time to stop malingering', but with simple joy that your creativity is waking up. Instead of bludgeoning it with an immediate deadline or word-count schedule, welcome it with gratitude and, perhaps, a celebratory biscuit.

As the life stress dissipates or your health improves or whatever threw you off the horse retreats and you can feel your creative brain waking up, you can think about getting back to your writing again.

Accept that it will take a bit of time to get back to wherever you were before the life event forced the break. You will have lost momentum, good habits may take work to be re-established and you may find that your old fears have grown in strength while you have been away from your work. As ever, the only way through these troubles is by writing and the very best complement to daily practice is compassion. Be nice to yourself and nice to your writing. It has been waiting patiently for you and it always will.

15

SWITCH UP

In this section I want to talk about change. We can all be a little bit frightened of change (please say it's not just me!) or we can be set in ways of doing things, ways of thinking. As a writer, you will be learning and growing all the time – that is why it is such a fascinating and exciting pursuit. So, first off, accept this fact. Embrace it!

Next, don't be alarmed if 'your' process changes over the years or even from book-to-book. Bestselling romantic comedy author Lani Diane Rich described how 'each book requires something different' and she has written ten of the things. Rather than getting more and more deeply set for each book, Lani is flexible enough to let each project dictate what it requires from her.

Another thing to be wary of as you gain experience is the urge to mess with your way of doing things just for the sake of it. Or, far more likely, because you read about how such-and-such writes six books a year and is making a gazillion pounds and you want to emulate their success. There is nothing wrong with trying out tips and advice, but you mustn't beat yourself up if they don't work for you. Or if they don't magically turn you into a different person (spoiler: they won't).

Even though I love reading writing advice (so much I even wrote a whole book of the stuff!) I found this sentiment immensely liberating. It's okay if trying to change your own process doesn't work. It's okay if you don't seem to have a set process and it alters from book to book. It's okay if you forget all the stuff that works for you and flounder for months before remembering how you do this thing. It's all okay. Nothing is permanent – not in life and not in writing.

I have lost count of the number of times I have had to relearn that writing first thing is my best time and that my happiness (and productivity) soars when I do it.

So, with those caveats in mind, here are some ideas for shaking up your writing routine. Sometimes we carry certain beliefs about ourselves and our creative processes which are actually holding us back and preventing us from finding new brilliant ways of working.

If you think you need three hours of total peace and quiet (empty diary, empty house) in which to write, challenge yourself to write in a coffee shop or while waiting in the car for your kids to finish their football practice.

If you think you can't write in the evenings (this is me!), try booking in ten-minute writing sprints on a couple of evenings and see how they go…

Instead of writing in silence, try playing music. Or vice versa.

Shake things up by reading outside your usual genre choices.

Finally, the most important thing to take away from this is that we are all learning all of the time and it's positive when that learning forces us to change our ideas, processes, thoughts, and areas of interest.

Learning as a writer is essential (and one of the wonderful aspects of the craft – we will never know it all!) and it's good to stay open to new ideas, alternative ways of doing things, and aspects of the craft (and process) of writing that we might not have considered. It is, however, your writing and writing life that matters. You are never learning the 'right' way to write, tell stories, or live a creative life; you are discovering your own way to do these things. Be confident in your own instincts to say 'this works for me' or 'this makes sense to me' and 'this doesn't'.

If you were academically able at school it can be difficult to embrace this; our self-doubt urges us to find the 'A grade' method or ethos, but when it comes to creative writing there is no such thing. Truly, there are no rules, only guidelines, and all that matters is the finished book, not *how* it was written.

16

YOU CAN DO THIS

I am going to give you a permission slip. It reads: 'You are a writer.'

So many of us are waiting to be 'allowed' to call ourselves writers or to put pen to paper. If we already write, we are waiting to be 'proper writers' or to be good enough to enter competitions or submit to agents or join that fancy writing class. I'm going to cut through all of that right here, right now.

You are allowed.

You are worthy.

You are a writer.

There is no special gated community where everything is easy and the money pours from the sky and the floor is littered with awards and film deals.

There is no place at which you feel you have 'made it'.

There is no point at which you stop worrying about the current book you are working on and exactly what happens next or whether it is any good/good enough.

There is no magical place, post-publication when you

turn into a super-confident writer who is totally comfortable and happy with their ability and work.

Every single finished book is a struggle and a triumph and is merely abandoned (the knowledge that it could be better/still isn't right or perfect haunts every writer, every time).

But, and here is the good news; if there is no shining 'after' to counteract the wasteland of 'before', that means all there is *is the writing*. The daily work. The being a writer. The thinking up stories. The day dreaming. The delicious research. The learning.

That is all there is for any of us and you are invited to join in.

So, take a piece of paper. If you prefer your invitation to come from me, consider it extended (with my warm wishes and a free hug if we ever meet in person!).

But you can write down whatever you like on your piece of paper. You can write, 'I am an author'. 'I am creative'. 'I am a writer.' 'I write.'

Whatever resonates with you. Now put that paper somewhere you won't lose it, but will see it regularly. In your wallet or on your desk or bedside table.

You have chosen. Right here and right now, you have chosen.

I remember my dear friend Keris stopping me when I was mid-whine with the words, 'at some point, you just have to decide you are good enough.'.

I had been moaning, not for the first time, that I was worried that my writing wasn't literary enough for my professors (I was doing my masters in Creative Writing at the time, striving for the validation I craved), I was frightened my agent wouldn't like my latest book or that I should try to write in this way or this way…

Her words hit me like a ten-ton truck. Like a bolt from the blue. Like a sock full of pennies.

At some point, if I ever wanted to be free of this continual self-doubt and second-guessing and terrible neediness, I was going to have to decide that I was good enough. That I deserved to be a writer. Not that I was instantly amazing and deserved success, not that I deserved to be universally adored, but that my words, my writing, my voice, my stories were worth creating. For myself.

And that, my friends, is the moment I began to choose myself. To write for myself. From that point on, while not always easy, I knew that I was going to stick at this writing thing, that I was willing and able to write about the worlds in my head, and that the tools I already had would just have to be enough.

I humbly suggest you do the same.

AFTERWORD

I've included everything that I have learned over the last ten years of writing 'seriously'. And I do mean Everything.

This is deliberate as I can't know which tip or anecdote will be the one to hit home for you. I hope it isn't too overwhelming, though, and I want to reiterate that you must take whatever works for you and discard the rest.

Don't try to implement too many new strategies at once and don't get discouraged if something that used to work ceases to be effective. Writing regularly and producing finished books is not easy. The rules (write lots, finish stuff) are simple but difficult to execute.

This is an ongoing process of discovery, learning and re-learning. It's okay – normal, even – to adjust your writing routine as life/the current book/your experience dictates. Don't think of it as getting to some mythical place where every day will be easy and joyful, but do appreciate those days which are. Celebrate your small wins every single day so that your writing work is filled with positivity and, most importantly, know that you are a writer and you are doing the exact same thing (and feeling the same self-doubt) as every single one of your writing heroes.

You are one of us, now; welcome!

READY FOR THE NEXT STEP?

Stop Worrying; Start Selling

The introvert author's guide to marketing

Do you want to sell more books? Terrified at the prospect of marketing and 'self promo'?

I felt exactly the same way... Until I changed my mindset around marketing, money and selling my work.

A practical and supportive guide to taking control of your success as an author and building your readership.

Don't give into the starving artist myth: Stop Worrying and Start Selling today!

'An incredibly helpful companion for the reluctant marketer, the new writer, and the veteran writer looking to up their game.'

— WENDY HEARD, AUTHOR OF *THE KILL CLUB*

ABOUT THE AUTHOR

Sarah is a bestselling author and host and creator of the Worried Writer podcast.

The backlist episodes and all show notes are available on the Worried Writer website. For extras and giveaways, please sign up to the mailing list.

Sarah's fiction includes the magical *The Language of Spells* and the dual narrative (part historical, part psychological thriller), *In The Light of What We See*.

Sarah lives in rural Scotland with her children and husband. She drinks too much tea, loves the work of Joss Whedon, and is the proud owner of a writing shed.

I love to connect with readers - please get in touch!
www.worriedwriter.com

facebook.com/theworriedwriter
twitter.com/sarahrpainter
instagram.com/sarahpainterbooks

RECOMMENDED READING

Rising Strong, Brené Brown

The Power of Habit, Charles Duhrigg

Lifelong Writing Habit, Chris Fox

Big Magic, Elizabeth Gilbert

On Writing, Stephen King

Bird By Bird, Anne Lamott

Business For Authors, Joanna Penn

Motivation For Creative People, Mark McGuinness

The 7 Secrets of the Prolific, Hillary Rettig

Writing into the Dark, Dean Wesley Smith

ACKNOWLEDGMENTS

This book would not exist if I hadn't discovered Joanna Penn's wonderful podcast, *The Creative Penn*, and decided that starting my own podcast would be 'good for me'. I had no idea how right I was... The encouragement and friendship from the listeners, and the wonderful advice and support I have received from my brilliant guests, has transformed my writing life. Thank you so much to everyone who listens, chats on Twitter, sends me messages and emails – I appreciate being a part of our little community so very much.

A special thank you to the authors who have given their time to be on the podcast – you all rock!

Also, thank you to all the readers and listeners who encouraged me to write this book. I truly hope it is helpful. Do let me know!

Finally, a metric ton of gratitude to my wonderful beta readers:

Jennie Hughes, Keris Stainton,
Laura N, Sheena Cundy,
Marie Madigan, Sarah Thorogood,
Claire Jennings, Hannah Mines

FICTION BY SARAH PAINTER

The Language of Spells
The Secrets of Ghosts
The Garden of Magic

In The Light of What We See
Beneath The Water

The Lost Girls

The Night Raven: Crow Investigations Book One
The Silver Mark: Crow Investigations Book Two
The Fox's Curse: Crow Investigations Book Three
The Pearl King: Crow Investigations Book Four